PENGUIN BOOKS

WAITING GAMES

Steve and Ruth Bennett are the authors of numerous books designed to help busy parents spend quality time with their children. Their titles include *Cabin Fever: 202 Activities for Turning Rainy Days, Snow Days, and Sick Days into Great Days* and *Kitchen Time: 202 Activities for Entertaining Your Child While You Cook.* They also penned the best-selling *365 TV-Free Activities You Can Do With Your Child* and *Kick the TV Habit: A Simple Program for Changing Your Family's Television Viewing and Video Game Habits.*

Steve has written more than fifty books on parenting, the environment, business management, and microcomputing. The former president of a technical publishing company, he holds a master's degree in regional studies from Harvard University.

Ruth is an illustrator and landscape architect who has designed public parks and playgrounds in a number of cities in the United States. She holds a master's degree in landscape architecture from the University of Virginia.

The Bennetts live with their two children, Audrey and Noah, in Cambridge, Massachusetts.

Steve and Ruth Bennett

WAITING GAMES

202 Instant Activities for Turning Time to Spare into Time to Share

PENGUIN BOOKS

PENGUIN BOOKS
Published by the Penguin Group
Penguin Books USA Inc., 375 Hudson Street,
New York, New York 10014, U.S.A.
Penguin Books Ltd, 27 Wrights Lane,
London W8 5TZ, England
Penguin Books Australia Ltd, Ringwood,
Victoria, Australia
Penguin Books Canada Ltd, 10 Alcorn Avenue,
Toronto, Ontario, Canada M4V 3B2
Penguin Books (N.Z.) Ltd, 182–190 Wairau Road,
Auckland 10, New Zealand

Penguin Books Ltd, Registered Offices:
Harmondsworth, Middlesex, England

First published in Penguin Books 1995

3 5 7 9 10 8 6 4 2

LIBRARY OF CONGRESS CATALOGING-IN-PUBLICATION DATA
Bennett, Steven J., 1951–
Waiting games : 202 instant activities for turning time to spare
into time to share / Steve and Ruth Bennett.
p. cm.
Includes index.
ISBN 0 14 02.3911 1
1. Games. 2. Amusements. I. Bennett, Ruth (Ruth Loetterle)
II. Title.
GV1201.B474 1995
790.1—dc20 94-42488

Printed in the United States of America
Set in Adobe ITC Garamond Light
Designed by Kate Nichols and Virginia Norey

Acknowledgments

Lots of brainstorming went into this book, and we're grateful to a number of people for sharing their wonderful ideas for waiting game activities. In particular, we'd like to thank Stacey Miller for her terrific contribution to our work; we didn't have to wait long to get a gaggle of games from her once we put out the call. Pete Scisco offered a lot of clever activity ideas, too, and we're deeply indebted to him for sharing his time and thoughts. Rich Freierman, an old waiting game master, offered a lot of neat ideas, too.

Caroline White, our editor, patiently waited for the manuscript to sail in the door. We thank her for putting up with our own version of "author waiting games." Thanks to Kathryn Court, too, our publisher, for her patience and support. Hats off to the Penguin design team for their work on the cover and interior of the book.

In addition, we thank Lynn Chu and Glen Hartley, our agents, for making this project possible.

Finally, we'd like to express our appreciation to the most patient people on the planet—our children, Audrey and Noah, who endured the time we put into creating another book. Thanks, kids.

Contents

16. Bumble Bee, Bumble Bee

17. Car Collectors

18. Car Talk

19. Career Curiosity

20. Changing Rooms

21. Changing Scenery

22. Checkout Features

23. Cloud Masters

24. Coin Games (Little Kids)

25. Coin Games (Older Kids)

26. Colorific

27. Countathon

28. Crazy Colors

29. Crazy Frozen Dinners

30. Crazy Street Signs

31. Crystal Ball

32. Describe That Food

33. Designer Coiffures

34. Dino Palates

35. Dinosaur Safari

36. Doctor, Doctor

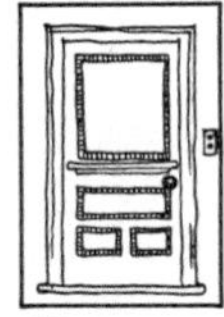

37. Door-to-Door Sales Pitches

38. Easy Category Game

39. Events in History

40. Everyday Heroes

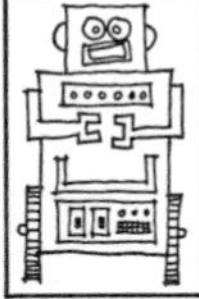

41. Everything Machine

42. Family Award

43. Fender-to-Fender Football

44. Find the Shape

45. Flying Colors Meal

46. Food-Free Aisles

47. Form Equals Function?

48. Fresh off the Press

49. Garage Sale

50. Geo Wizards

51. Geo Word Game

52. Ghost Runners

53. Great Answering Machine Tapes

54. Guess That Creature

55. Habitats

56. Hand Signals

57. Head in the Sand

58. Historical Interview

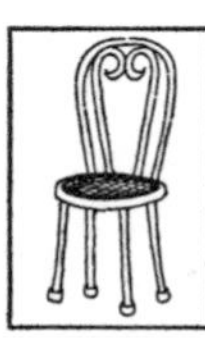

59. Historical Tour

60. How Many Words?

61. How to . . .

62. How to Be Brave

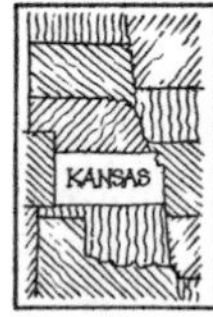

63. Howdy, Neighbor

64. Humdinger

65. If the Walls Could Talk

66. Instant Grown-ups

67. Intergalactic Interview

68. Invisible Kids

69. Item Counter

70. Just Hangin' Around

71. Kid Pix

72. Kids' Book of Home Remedies

73. Know Your Postal Codes

74. Know Your Vitamins

75. Landmark Locations

76. Landscape Architects

77. Letter Starters

78. Life Without Laws

79. Lights Out

80. Like Night and Day

81. Line Math

82. Line Races

83. Lion's Paws and Gaping Maws

84. Make a Meal

85. Make an Acronym

86. Mechanical Advantage

87. Meet the Olympiad

88. Menu Math

89. Menu Word Games

90. Modern Conveniences

91. Month, Please

92. More Coin Games

93. Most Important Numbers

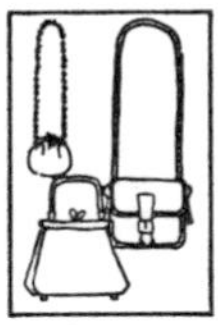
94. Mosts and Leasts

95. Mountain Climbing

96. My Strangest Case

97. Name Game

98. Name That Job

99. Name the Buildings

100. Neighbor-hood Awards

101. Night and Day

102. No Countries

103. No Peeking

104. Object of the Story

105. Off-the-Cuff

106. Oh, the Times!

107. On the Other Hand . . .

108. One-Inch Adventures

109. Opposites

110. Origins of Holidays

111. Origins of Things

112. Out of This World

113. Pace It Out

114. Peaks of the World

115. Pet Talk

116. Pictures by Request

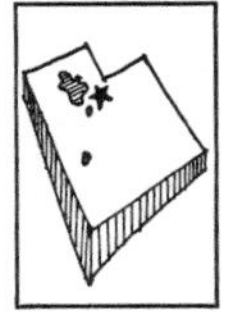
117. Place That City

118. Places Unknown

119. Point Counterpoint (Little Kids)

120. Point Counterpoint (Older Kids)

121. Presidents Past and Present

122. Prove It!

123. Quick Caricatures

124. Quick Titles

125. Rename the Eatery

126. Repealing Newton's Law

127. Report from Washington

128. Restaurant Counts

129. Restaurant Groups

130. Rhyme Time

131. Roving Encyclopedia

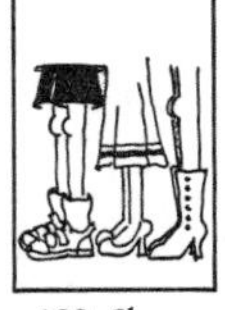
132. Shoes Game

133. Shopping Cart Organizer

134. Short to Tall

135. Sign Jumbles

136. Sign Language

137. Signs and Stories

138. Sky Watchers

139. Solar System Kids

140. Song-maker

141. Soundalikes

142. Sounds of Cities

143. Space Odyssey

144. Space Voyage

145. Speedy Word-Guessers

146. Sports Matching

147. Step-by-Step

148. Sub-terraneans

149. Sugar Packet Fun

150. Sum It Up

151. Super Math

152. Surprise Drawings

153. Sur-viving the Stone Age

154. Sweet Magic

155. Take a Trip

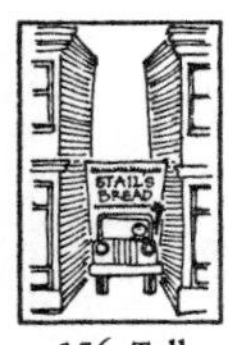

156. Tall Tales

157. Team Efforts

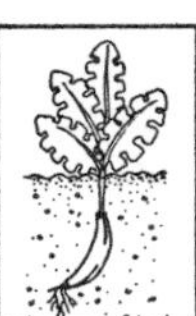

158. They Grow on Trees

159. This Place in Time

160. Time Travelers

161. Time Zones

162. Touch of Gold

163. Tour Masters

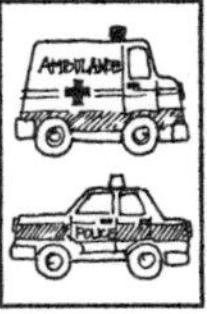

164. Traffic Cops

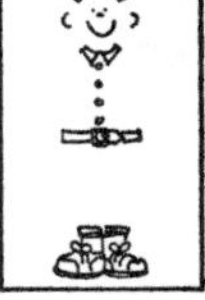

165. Upside Down

166. Waiting Room Detectives

167. Waiting Room Hot and Cold

168. Waiting Room Scouts

169. Waiting Room with a View

170. Waiting Words

171. Waitperson of the Hour

172. Water, Water Everywhere

173. Weigh-In

174. What a Character!

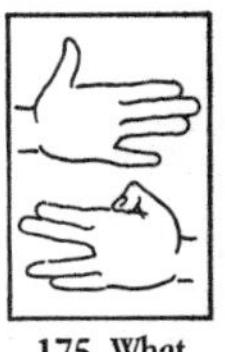

175. What Am I?

176. What Am I Made Of?

177. What Doesn't Belong (Little Kids)

178. What Doesn't Belong (Older Kids)

179. What Kind of Food

180. What Would Happen if Everybody Did It?

181. What Would They Do?

182. What's Around the Corner?

183. What's for Dinner?

184. What's Next?

185. Where Do I Live?

186. Where Does It Come From?

187. Where's the State?

188. Which Event Came First?

189. Which Thing Came First?

190. Who Did It?

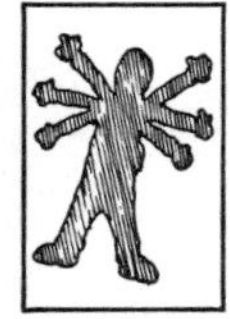

191. Who Knows What Fun Lurks . . .

192. Who's Next?

193. Window Theater

194. Window Watchers

195. Windows on the World

Introduction

From Waiting Time to Quality Time

- The ticket line at the movie theater, the circus, or some other event has set a world record—for slowness.

- You're stuck in rush hour traffic with your son or daughter. The only thing that seems to be moving quickly is your kid's tide of impatience.

- You and your child have waited forty-five minutes for a pediatrician's appointment, and the doctor is still "with another patient."

- The waiter has just informed you that things are "backed up" in the kitchen—shouldn't be more than, oh, twenty minutes or so before your kids' burgers will be out.

- Your child is waiting for a ride to a school event or playgroup. The driver will arrive in fifteen minutes, unless she's stuck in traffic.

These are the situations that try parents' souls. But they can also be great opportunities to prove that "wait" doesn't have to be a four-letter word; in fact, it's really a three-letter word in disguise: FUN. All it takes is a quick change of mindset and some creative ideas. This book will help with the creative ideas, so you can adopt a positive attitude whenever waiting time is on your mind.

Waiting Games is designed to show you how to transform minutes to spare into productive and pleasant interludes, whether you and your children find yourselves waiting your turn at the checkout counter, in traffic, at a restaurant, at the bus stop, at the supermarket, at the doctor's office, or even at home—all of the times when the clock seems to be dragging its hands and *your* hands are filled with kids eager to be doing something else.

Each activity is designed to be done "on the spot," with no preparation or elaborate props (at most, some require pencil and notepad, which you'll probably take along anyway when you make an excursion with your kids). We've classified the activities two ways: first, by suggested usage, second, by activity type.

The suggested usage is listed underneath the activity number that appears in the pocket watch. The usage categories include:

Anytime, Anyplace. Here's a collection of lifesavers that will work for parents in most waiting situations. These activities can be done at the drop of a hat, indoors or outdoors, with whatever materials are around, and within whatever time you have to spare.

By Appointment. Whether at the doctor's, dentist's, motor vehicle registry, car dealership, or service station, you and your kids can use these games and activities to take your minds off the wait (or the fears of a doctor appointment), and put them where they should be—on having fun!

Gridlock Busters. When the expressway becomes a "distressway," and it takes forever to get from "A" to "B," these games and activities will help you and your kids forget that you're stuck in traffic.

Shopping and Erranding. Tired of arguing about whether or not to buy your child every candy bar in the checkout line at the supermarket and other stores? Then try these activities, and find out how peaceful and entertaining waiting to pay can be.

Waiting in Line. Ideas for entertaining your kids before the entertainment begins. Easy games that can be done whenever you have to queue up for tickets or admission to an event.

Waiting to be Served. How do you keep growling stomachs from translating into growling kids at a restaurant? Try the activities in this category; they're designed to be used when you're waiting to be seated, waiting for your order to be taken, or waiting for your food to arrive.They work in your own kitchen, too!

Walking There. Outdoor activities meant to be done when you're "hoofing it," say, from your home to a park or from your car to a school event.

Underneath the illustration on each page you'll notice the second category which describes what the activity is all about. The activity types include:

Curtain Call. Suggestions for role-playing everything from friends and relatives to insects and dinosaurs, and demonstrating theatrical, oratorical, and persuasive speaking skills.

Doodles to Go. On-the-spot drawing and other games, such as easy caricatures and "surprise drawings," that require only a pad and pencil.

Instant Games. Easy guessing and other types of games in which your kids make predictions (like how many patrons will enter a restaurant in the next five minutes), locate words in numbers on signs and posters, play variations on charades, make change without looking, and carry out other engaging actions.

Observe the World. "Find it" games (like looking out the window for trucks of a certain color) that encourage children to take a closer look at their surroundings and hone their powers of observation.

Reporter-at-Large. Activities that allow you and your child to take turns being a reporter and a subject for an interview. Just roll up a piece of paper or magazine, and you'll have an instant microphone for interviewing subjects ranging from astronauts to animals that have escaped from the zoo!

What an Imagination! Activities that involve storytelling and language arts, such as rhyming and word matching, and fantasy, such as describing what a storybook character might do when visiting the dentist.

What if. . . . What would your kids do if they woke up one morning and found they were only an inch tall? Here's a collection of whimsical activities designed to set your children's creative powers on full throttle by asking them to describe what would happen if improbable situations actually came to pass.

Wise Kids. Activities that involve guessing, creative brainstorming, or demonstrating a knowledge of academic subjects such as math, history, geography, and the sciences.

Word Wizards. A compilation of quick-play word games that draw on and build your child's language and reading skills. Activities include finding all the words that can be made using the letters in a restaurant's name, making up clever acronyms, or distinguishing made-up words from highfalutin real ones.

Once you've perused the book, you'll have a good idea about which types of activities are best suited to your children's ages, abilities, and interests—and which are most likely to provide "life support" for the waiting situations in which you most often find yourself (check the index for a complete listing of activities by usage categories and activity types). As the old saying goes, the best time to make an escape plan is before you need one. Same with *Waiting Games* activities. Get acquainted with the activities before you need them.

If, for instance, you're about to pay a visit to the pediatrician or dentist, check out the "By Appointment" activities (you'll find them all listed in the index), and pick out a few that you know will work especially well in your doctor's office. Ditto for a trip to the supermarket or a car ride that's likely to take you through slow-moving or bumper-to-bumper traffic.

While you can flip open the book and find something that meets your needs at the moment, there's nothing like the security of knowing that you're always ready—with waiting games in hand—whenever you might have to wait.

After exploring the activities in this book, you'll quickly discover that, with a few "tweaks and twists," you can easily modify your favorites to fit into any waiting context. For example, if you're stuck in traffic instead of waiting in a checkout line, you can easily turn "Aisle Scavenger Hunt" into a "Highway Scavenger Hunt," or transform "Shopping Cart Organizer" into "Backseat Organizer."

Beyond always having some activities "in your pocket" (you'll probably want to take the book with you to provide a quick infusion of ideas), there are a few considerations you ought to keep in mind before trying our ideas with your kids:

Think Safety. As with all activities, these call for parents to exercise their normal good judgment as kids explore the world of a waiting room, count items in a busy store, or look for clues on a neighborhood or city street. It's easy to get absorbed in the games, so keep a watchful eye as you would whenever you travel about town, shop, or run errands with your child.

Keep Competition Down. In all of our books, we recommend deemphasizing the competitive aspects of play. If an activity requires keeping score, try playing cooperatively when you can—everyone scores for the group as a whole. Or try to focus kids on topping their own previous scores. When a winner is necessary, congratulate *everyone* on his or her fine play and move on to another round.

Be flexible. Encourage your child to devise new rules for the games or variations on what we propose—except for safety considerations, there is no "right" way to do any of the activities in this book. By encouraging your child to devise creative alternatives, 202 activities will quickly become 404, 606, or even more things to do!

Now, there's no reason to wait a second longer for the fun to begin!

Steve and Ruth Bennett
Cambridge, Massachusetts
September 1994

WAITING GAMES

Action Codes

When you get to a red light, what do you do? Why, clap three times, of course!

Anytime, Anyplace

Make a list of things you might see while you're waiting. If you're walking or riding, you might include: trucks, traffic lights, stop signs, buses, bicycles, trees, a pedestrian, a car beeping its horn, and so on. If you're waiting in line, you might list: a baby, a knapsack, someone holding tickets, a new ticket line opening up, and so on.

Then, your child decides on an action for everyone to do each time he or she sees something on the list. Perhaps every time you spot a truck you sing the ABC song, every time you see a bicycle you snap your fingers, when you see a baby you pat your head, and when a customer arrives to stand at the back of the line you jump twice.

If your child is feeling tricky, he or she might carry out the actions and let you guess the "secret" code. How many hops will it take you to realize that hopping means a UFO has just landed in the middle of the street?

Aisle Scavenger Hunt

Shopping and Erranding

While you're searching the supermarket aisles for food items to put into your cart, your super-sleuth child can scout for other must-fina groceries in the same aisle.

Scan the aisles quickly, and then compose an on-the-spot list of things for your child to find, based on what you believe will be there. For instance, if you're in the canned goods aisle, you might challenge your child to find fruit cocktail, peas and carrots, and pineapple rings. Or in the cookie row, your child's mission might be to discover the vanilla wafers, shortbread cookies, and gingersnaps.

Place a time limit on the scavenger hunt; for example, your child might have two minutes to spot the items in each aisle (or until you've finished your shopping, whichever comes first). Encourage older children to guess whether scavenger hunt items are part of this trip's purchases. No, you probably *don't* need eight brands ot spaghetti sauce for tonight's dinner!

All Day, All Night

What if your children never had to sleep (because they received one-of-a-kind pills as part of a scientific experiment)? Ask how they would:

Anytime, Anyplace

Spend their time at night when everybody else was asleep. What would it be like to have the whole house to themselves? What would your kids do if they got bored with all that time on their hands?

Relax. Since your kids wouldn't be able to forget about the events of the day and refresh their minds by sleeping, how would they unwind and get ready to face a new day?

Explain to other people why they didn't have to sleep. What would your kids do if they were invited to slumber parties, or if they went away to overnight camp? How would your kids explain why they didn't dream?

Once your kids have thought about what it might be like to never have to sleep again, pose this question: If you could be part of this experiment, would you sign up?

Alphabet Chase

Anytime, Anyplace

If you ever see the words *race* and *letter* in the same sentence, chances are you aren't talking about the mail. But you might be playing this game.

The object of the game is to see who can reach the end of the alphabet first using letters found on billboards, street signs, store displays, magazine covers, or other printed materials. Players must gather their letters in alphabetical order. That "Appleby's Cafe" sign, for example, offers an *a*, *b*, and *c*.

If you're stuck somewhere without access to street signs or billboards, use anything else in view that has letters—posters, pamphlets, and the like.

If you're in traffic, let one team or child use the signs out the right window, while another child or team uses the signs on the left. Or, the youngest kids might get to use any kind of sign, while older kids have to use store signs. From time to time, one team will get stuck while another moves ahead or catches up—there seem to be plenty of *p*s, but not a lot of *q*s out there!

Observe the World

Animal Crackers

Anytime, Anyplace

Every adult remembers being scared of the monster at night that turns out to be a jacket hanging over the back of a chair. This activity lets kids make up their own strange creatures from the things they see all around them.

To get started, pick a building, a piece of furniture, or a vehicle and describe the animal it looks like. A cement truck might look like a hippopotamus. A train might look like a big snake or a gigantic worm.

Kids don't have to stick with everyday names for their fantastic creatures. Encourage them to come up with new species. "Dumptruckeros" is tough to say, but it's a harmless dirt-eating creature. The long-necked "Craneoton" swings its small head above the tall building, feeding on the vegetation there. Inside, the quiet "Crooked-Leg Chair Bird" sits calmly around Table Lake. In the background, the sounds of the hard-to-find "Ruby-Throated Radio Wingding" drift through the doctor's office.

You and your kids can feel free to go crackers playing this animal make-up game because there aren't any crumbs to make a mess.

Observe the World

Bag It?

Shopping and Erranding

It's a burning question, and it's on the minds of all baggers at the supermarket checkout: paper or plastic? See how well your child can handle various aspects of the bagger's job.

As you wait in line at the checkout, see whether your child can guess which customers will want paper bags and which ones will ask for plastic bags. Your child might earn two points for each correctly assessed customer.

Once your child gets to be an ace at determining customers' bag preferences, he or she can try to predict how many bags each order will require. Your child can also watch for "world bagging records": What's the greatest number of bags an order requires? What's the quickest time for filling a bag? What's the greatest number of items that can fit into a bag?

Finally, you can challenge your child to guess which items will wind up in the same bag when it's your turn to pay for your purchases. Hopefully, the predictions about the watermelon, potatoes, and eggs in the same bag won't come true!

Balanced Nutrition

These days there's a lot of talk about the new food "pyramid" (see diagram). Can your child use it to create a balanced

Anytime, Anyplace

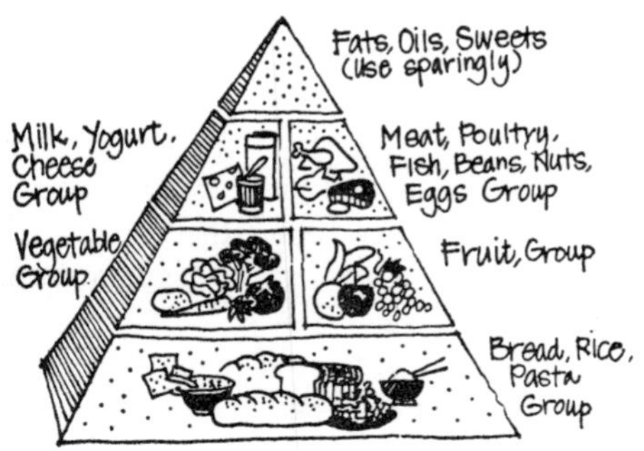

Begin by suggesting various food items, such as bread, chicken, and cottage cheese. Ask your child which group each item belongs to. Then ask for examples of a balanced menu for a whole day, starting with breakfast and ending with dinner. You can also play a zany version and see if your child can envision the *worst* possible diet for a day, or perhaps even modify the food chart so that it's appropriate for pets.

Let's see now, fifteen helpings of ice cream per day? Dairy, right? Not exactly what the pyramid builders had in mind!

Beat the Band

Gridlock Busters

Everybody loves music, and it's a great way to pass the time. But you don't have to turn on the car radio to enjoy a tune.

First, get everybody in the car to agree on a tune. It should be familiar enough so that all players know the melody. For very young children, you can use simple songs, like "Twinkle, Twinkle Little Star." Older kids might want to use a popular song from the radio.

Each person then chooses an instrument that he or she can mimic. The drums are almost always the most popular choice, so kids can take turns being the percussion for different songs. Other instruments that are easy to mimic include the tuba (oompah), flute (toot toot), the trumpet (doo dee doo), and the electric guitar (wah wah dah dah dah).

Each player should make a sound like the instrument he or she has chosen. When the band is ready, launch into your number. The fun really starts when the band members improvise solos. Then you're really jamming!

Curtain Call

Become a Collector

Anytime, Anyplace

The world is full of people who collect coins, stamps, toy trains, and various odds and ends. Why not encourage your child to join their ranks while you wait?

Your child's collection can be useful (say, recipes or coupons from the supermarket) or informational (perhaps pamphlets about health from the doctor's office or cavity prevention from the dentist's).

Also, while your child is waiting, he or she can begin to organize his or her "collectibles." Perhaps the items can be sorted alphabetically, by color, by shape, or by subject. Once your child has finished sorting his or her stash, see whether you can figure out the organizational method.

Then challenge your child to find the most effective way, the most complicated way, and the most creative way to catalog his or her collection. Remember, the longer you wait, the more your child will have to organize, and the greater the possibilities!

Big Wheels, Little Wheels

Anytime, Anyplace

Wheels, you might say, make the world go round. This seek-and-find game goes one better: it makes time go by fast.

To play, mom or dad says "big wheel" and kids must find the biggest wheel they can see from the window of the car, or from wherever they're waiting. If more than one child is playing, each child should go in turn from youngest to oldest. See how many big wheels can be found. See who can find the biggest of the big. Then try it with the smallest wheel.

Kids can use their imaginations in this game if they get a chance. For example, if your child sees a plane flying above, that can count as a big wheel (when it's on the ground), or as a small wheel (when it's in the air).

If you're waiting somewhere that doesn't have vehicles that can readily be seen, your children can play the game in their minds. All they have to do is name vehicles that roll on big or little wheels, and give an appropiate clue.

This game is sure to get the fun rolling during any wait!

Observe the World

Bistro Spy

The old "I Spy" game can be a sanity saver when your kids are ready to eat but the restaurant is on its own schedule. Here are a few variations that can turn that waiting time into instant fun time.

Waiting to Be Served

If you're waiting for a table to be cleared, start off a "spy" session by suggesting various objects in the entry area, such as the coat rack, the maitre d's microphone, the cash register, plants, and various decorations. Get creative with older kids by offering cryptic clues. For instance, you might say, "I spy something with a mouth that occasionally opens and swallows flat, rectangular green objects and round, shiny disks" (the cash register).

Once you're seated, use objects around the table, such as art on the menu, place mats, napkins, advertising placards, art on the walls, and so on. Don't forget subtle items such as wallpaper, designs in the carpet, and silverware patterns.

Won't everyone be happy when you can call out, "I spy something coming from the kitchen and headed our way!"

Observe the World

12 Body Language

Anytime, Anyplace

Why are your kids rubbing their stomachs and tapping their heads? Because, they're speaking in a secret code (they're actually concurring that it's time for an ice-cream break).

You can get in on the action, too, by helping your children devise a code language that can involve words, hand signs, and various types of body language. Start off simple, with a substitute for "yes" and "no." Perhaps patting the head means "yes" and pointing to the nose means "no." Ask a series of yes/no questions, such as, "Is your name Madeline?" "Do you like chocolate?" "Do we live on earth?" Rattle off the questions as quickly as you can, seeing if your kids can keep the hand signals straight.

Next, up the challenge by substituting body language for common words. For instance, pointing to an elbow might mean "table," and waving twice might mean "book." So you might say, "Please pass the green [wave twice] on the [point to elbow].

See how many substitutions you and your kids can devise. When you're done, you may be able to have a complete conversation without opening your mouths!

Body Mix-Ups

Anytime, Anyplace

Get your kids laughing, and their minds off the waiting, with crazy body combinations. This game would even get a giggle out of Dr. Frankenstein.

All you need to get started are the two most inventive words in English: "Imagine that . . ." For example, say, "Imagine that your ears were your nose?" Use your fingers to point to the mix-up. The picture kids get in their minds—or the one you get in yours—will have you laughing in no time.

The fun gets even better when everyone starts talking about the implications of the mix-ups: "I guess you could hear smells!", or, "Then you could smell music!"

You can take the game even further by asking your kids to think of special jobs that would be suited for a person with wacky mixed-up body parts. How about this one: If you had eyes where your toes are, you'd easily find all those marbles that have rolled under the refrigerator!

What an Imagination!

Book Reviewers

Anytime, Anyplace

One of the best things about reading a book is sharing it with others. If you have a few minutes to fill, let your child give you the book he or she has read most recently by offering an on-the-spot review.

Your child first tells you the title of the book and fills you in on the characters. Then he or she sketches the plot and offers his or her opinion about the work. He or she can also answer your questions, such as: What was the best part about the book? Which characters did you like the most? What was the most interesting part? The funniest? The saddest? Would you recommend the book to others?

If you've read the book as well, then you and your child can brainstorm ideas for improving it. For example, maybe you can invent a new character, an exciting plot twist, an exotic setting, or even a new ending.

Who knows, maybe Pooh will open his own honey factory or Huck Finn will eventually find his way to the Nile River!

What an Imagination!

Brush Twice a Day!

What if sharks got toothaches; who would they turn to for help? Perhaps dentists like yours.

By Appointment

As you sit in your dentist's waiting room, create a story about the time that a shark came for an appointment, and how difficult it was to identify the cavity-laden culprit from among its fellow teeth. After you get the story line rolling, have your child explain to the shark how to prevent cavities in the future, which foods to avoid, why it's good to floss every day, and of course, the importance of brushing.

Sharks aren't the only critters in need of dental advice, though. Perhaps your child might want to describe strange encounters with camels, armadillos, and alligators who ignored the principles of good tooth care. Then there's always the Tyrannosaurus Rex whose fillings kept falling out!

In any case, use the zany opportunity to lighten things and defuse any of your child's anxieties. Your dentist will certainly be surprised when you relay some of his or her most unusual cases!

What an Imagination!

Bumble Bee, Bumble Bee

Anytime, Anyplace

The title of this activity takes its name from the childhood rhyme that always accompanies it in our house: "Bumble bee, bumble bee, I see something that you don't see, and the color of it is . . ."

The person who says the rhyme must choose a single object that's in plain sight. The other players, using only the object's color as a clue, must locate and name the item.

If you have a lot of time to pass, choose an object that's in plain sight but not at first obvious, such as a red hat worn by a model on a billboard. If the wait is short, or if you want a faster paced game, choose obvious objects, such as a building or a tree.

You can also give your kids clues as to how well they're doing by saying "cold" when they name something far away from the selected object, "warm" when they get closer, and "hot" when they're very close to the right pick.

Because it's based on colors, even very young children can play this game. And you might be surprised at what they notice in the world around them!

Observe the World

Car Collectors

17

Gridlock Busters

Former baseball star Reggie Jackson has a huge collection of vintage cars in his garage. Here's a way for your kids to collect their own fleet without ever swinging a bat.

While stopped at a traffic light, grab a pad and paper and sketch a quick grid. Put each child's name down the side. Along the top, list different kinds of vehicles. For example, you might write "cement mixer, dump truck, moving van, delivery truck, motorcycle, limousine, station wagon," and so on.

As you slowly make your way through traffic, kids keep their eyes peeled for the cars on the list. As they find one, they make a check next to their name in the appropriate box.

When you get to your destination, compare collections. Kids can try to complete their fleet by "trading." For example, if one child saw two dump trucks, he or she can swap the "extra" one for an extra station wagon that you or another child marked down.

You can keep the lists going until all of the squares are filled. After all, no serious collector wants a half-empty garage.

Observe the World

Car Talk

Walking There

If cars could talk, what would they say? You and your child can decide for yourselves next time you're out walking.

Take some time to notice the cars that pass by—pay special attention to the colors, sizes, shapes, and unusual features of the vehicles. Then ask your child to give an impromptu speech, in the character of one of the cars. For example, if your child playacts a minivan, he or she might say, "I'm a strong vehicle, and my favorite pastime is to take families for long drives and keep them safe."

After your child finishes the speech, you can ask him or her such questions as: "Can you describe the family that owns you?" "Who is the most interesting passenger you've ever driven?" "What's your favorite route to drive?" and "What's the farthest you've ever traveled?" (Your child answers all questions in character.)

Your child can also playact such vehicles as bicycles, trucks, vans, airplanes, or any other modes of transportation you see in your travels. Now, what do you suppose that skateboard is thinking?

Curtain Call

Career Curiosity

Anytime, Anyplace

If your child is still deciding what to be when he or she grows up, here's a waiting game activity that can help.

Your child pretends to be a grown-up with an exciting career, and you interview the "worker" to find out more about his or her job. Here are some questions you might consider asking: What is your job title? Where do you spent most of your time while you're working? What do you like best about your job? How did you train to do your job? What do you ususally wear while you're working? Do you work by yourself or do you work with other people? What equipment or tools do you use at work? What was your most exciting day ever on the job? and so on.

In case your child hasn't yet narrowed down possible future careers, here are some potential jobs he or she can "take on" while you're waiting: lion tamer, teacher, circus clown, astronaut, doctor, veterinarian, chef, mail carrier, and fire fighter. Perhaps your child will surprise you and choose your career, or that of another family member. There's no greater flattery than to have your child aspire to be like you when he or she grows up!

Reporter-at-Large

Changing Rooms

By Appointment

Here's an activity that will turn any waiting room into an amusement park for the mind. And you won't have to turn it upside down either!

The idea is to have your child focus on some aspect of the room and then close his or her eyes. You then alter something and see if he or she can figure out what's different. For example, let's say that the waiting room has a stack of magazines on a coffee table, and the top magazine happens to have a red cover. Have your child look in the vicinity of the table, then, while his or her eyes are closed, place a different magazine on top.

You can also rearrange coats on a coatrack, place a brochure backwards in a rack, or conduct other little bits of chicanery that won't cause anyone extra work to tidy up (you might suggest a rule that the room changer puts everything back the way it was after a round of guessing has taken place).

Say, do you suppose there's always been a mitten hanging on that ficus tree by the window?

Observe the World

Changing Scenery

Walking There

What will the street that you and your child are walking along look like three months from now? In six months? How about in ten months? Just ask your child, and you're likely to get a pretty interesting picture.

Name a season other than the current one, and ask your child to describe what he or she would be seeing along your walking path if it were that time of year. Say you want it to be wintertime. Your child might then tell you that there's just been a blizzard that's buried the street under six feet of snow, and you can barely see the tops of the chimneys. Or perhaps there's a snowman under construction in the yard next door, and if you look carefully, you can see a whole snow family lined up behind him!

Your child might also point out decorations that people have put up in anticipation of a holiday during the season you specify. Hmm, how many make-believe Fourth of July flags can your child count in March?

What an Imagination!

Checkout Features

Shopping and Erranding

Maybe you can't read all the magazines while you're waiting in the checkout line at the supermarket. But your child can certainly help you imagine what's inside the covers.

While you're in line, your child weaves a story that might go with the picture on the cover of a magazine that you point out. Perhaps the woman shown holding a kitten is an ambassador from another country, and she's here to tell us how the citizens of her home take special care of their pets. Or the family pictured on another cover will be the First Family of the United States sometime in the future.

Your young reporter can also tell you other stories based on the titles on magazine covers. Perhaps he or she can describe the new fall fashions, fifty ways to decorate with Jell-O, or the aliens that landed on the Empire State Building.

If you're up for a challenge, you can listen to your child's story and see whether you can match it with the "right" magazine. So which junior model is the new kid in your child's classroom?

What an Imagination!

Cloud Masters

Anytime, Anyplace

Should you have taken your umbrella today? Snow boots? Sunscreen? Just consult with your child meteorologist!

Ask your child about various weather phenomena, such as rain, snow, and the like. How does the rain get out of the clouds? What's the difference between rain and snow? And what kinds of clouds are most likely to produce rain (the dark puffy, or "cumulonimbus" variety, actually)? Why's the center of a hurricane, where things are almost calm, called the "eye"?

When you're done with your meteorology lesson, your expert weather reporter might actually do a customized forecast for wherever you're waiting. The forecast can include the current weather conditions, as well as short- and long-term predictions regarding sunshine, temperatures, wind direction and speed, and precipitation.

The forecast doesn't have to be all serious stuff, of course; it can include the zany as well. "Yes, it will be raining cats and dogs, so if you've been looking for a new pet, just wait till later this evening!"

Wise Kids

Coin Games (Little Kids)

Anytime, Anyplace

If you have a handful of coins and a tabletop nearby, then you have all you need to turn waiting time into a series of exciting coin games.

Drop your coins on the table, and ask your child to sort them according to type: quarters, dimes, nickels, and pennies. Then see whether your sorter can group together various coin combinations, such as two quarters and four dimes, six pennies and two nickels, three dimes and one penny, and so on.

You can also suggest that your child make coin patterns by lining up the coins in whichever order you specify—say, two pennies and a dime, followed by one penny and a dime—across the table. See whether your child can guess how many coins, or how many pattern sets, it will take to make a line from edge to edge. As your child gets better at the pattern game, increase the challenge by suggesting more complex patterns.

We've noticed another pattern; the more simple coin games you play, the faster the waiting time seems to fly!

Coin Games (Older Kids)

Anytime, Anyplace

In which year were most of the coins you have in your pocket or change purse minted? If your child has some free time on his or her hands, perhaps you can call for an investigation into this and other coin-related matters.

Empty your change pocket or purse onto a table (or, if you're at home, you might play the coin games on the floor instead). Then have your child sort the coins by dates. See how many pennies, nickels, dimes, and quarters you have that were printed during the year your child was born; the year that you (and other relatives and friends) were born; the year the current president of the United States was elected; the current year, and so on.

Then ask your child to find the "rarest" coin date, the shiniest coin, or the most "well-worn" coin. Perhaps your child will even find a fifty-cent piece if he or she looks hard enough. The game might seem like small change, but it can have a big payoff when it comes to transforming waiting time into fun time!

Colorific

Anytime, Anyplace

To a small child, the world is filled with color and motion. You can take advantage of those young eyes with this fun and easy game that builds on color recognition skills.

To play, an adult selects a color. Kids must then find and name as many objects as they can that are of the same color. Different hues can count as the same color. For example, brick red and fire-engine red can both be counted for red.

Older kids can combine colors to make another color. If, for example, you say "green," your child might say "the blue truck and the yellow sign" to make green. Mixing colors also makes it possible to have team play, in which groups of kids combine colors to make the target color. One player might find the blue truck, while his or her partner finds the yellow sign.

If your kids are familiar with the colors of the rainbow, you can inject that element into the game. See if they can find all of the rainbow colors before your wait is over. Wow—you don't even have to wait for a rainy day!

Observe the World

Countathon

Walking There

The attractions of your neighborhood or town are undoubtedly many—but they're almost certainly not too many for your child to count!

While you and your child are walking to an appointment or event, why not start counting the many things you encounter? Countables include: cars, bicycles, trees, signs, windows, roofs, chimneys, birds, sidewalk cracks, garages, flower beds, and doors. You and your child might also keep count of objects of various colors (beginning with the first color you see).

Perhaps the two of you can tally each category for five minutes and see which category boasts the most objects during that amount of time. Or, you and your child might keep separate tallies silently for a period of time and then see whether you come up with the same total.

So now, how does *this* waiting game add up?

Crazy Colors

Anytime, Anyplace

Did you ever consider what would happen if kids colored our world with crayons and watercolors, rather than the dull grays and reds that adults use in buildings and roads? Here's a way to splash some fun onto an otherwise drab wait—without carrying art supplies with you wherever you go.

To play, just pick an object and color it in your imagination. "See that bus over there?" you might ask. "What if we painted it purple with green spots?"

That's all you need to get kids moving down the street, "coloring" everything in their path. Add to their creations with your own suggestions. A moving escalator might have different colored stairs—maybe the stairs change color each time they go around!

One of our favorites is to paint all of the roads in different colors, then imagine what would happen if it rained while the paint was still wet. Now, talk about modern art!

Crazy Frozen Dinners

Shopping and Erranding

Have you heard of the Junior Shoppers' line of frozen food dinners? They include just about anything, in any combination, that your child can imagine!

As you're walking in the frozen food section of the supermarket, your child can see what types of items are really available and use them for inspiration. Perhaps your child can, in his or her mind's eye, combine various frozen food products and turn them into a whole meal that food manufacturers haven't yet thought of. For example, perhaps blueberries, ice cream, and potato puffs would make a wonderful frozen breakfast, while french fries, onion rings, and cake would be the perfect frozen dinner—for someone from another planet.

Your child can take crazy dinner-making a step further by selecting foods that haven't yet landed in the frozen food section. Perhaps he or she can devise a frozen chef's salad, complete with frozen lettuce, tomatoes, turkey, and dressing, or a sandwich complete with peanut butter, jelly, and bread. Now how's that for a thaw-it-and-eat-it meal?

What an Imagination!

Crazy Street Signs

Gridlock Busters

Stuck in traffic? Pass some time by turning work and road signs into wacky, funny messages.

To make the game challenging for all, suggest a couple of simple ground rules (after that, anything goes!). First off, a player can only change one word on the sign. Second, the word that gets changed must begin with the same letter as the word that takes its place. As an alternative, you might try substituting words that rhyme for the words in the sign.

Take the "Men at Work" sign over that manhole. That sign could become "Martians at Work." Or, that "No Trespassing" sign can become "No Trampolining" or "No Trapeze Acts." And that bothersome "No Parking Zone"; why not make it the "No Barking Zone"!

Excuse me, Bowser—can't you read the sign?

Observe the World

Crystal Ball

Anytime, Anyplace

Are your kids tired of waiting? Well, in the future there will be no such thing as waiting, because of the invention of the "Anti-Clock," a remarkable device that eliminates waiting time.

What else does the future have in store for us? Just ask your child about things like travel. Will wheels be a thing of the past? How fast will vehicles travel? What will power them?

How about foods? What will we eat and how will it be grown or created? What foods will no longer be around (will burgers and fries have gone the way of the dinosaur)? What form will the food be in?

Ask about other categories as well, such as medicine (an end to the common cold?), housing (buildings that change shape when you get tired of them?), sports (jet tag and high-altitude cloud hockey?), and clothing (indestructible garments that dirt won't stick to?).

Don't be surprised if you learn about an instant homework machine—that will probably be one of the first inventions of the twenty-first century!

What an Imagination!

Describe That Food

Waiting to be Served

The next time your kids are getting fidgety waiting for a restaurant meal, try this quick and easy guessing game.

One person thinks of a food—something that one of the family members has ordered, something on the menu, or any food that comes to mind—then gives clues as to its identity. If younger kids are playing, keep the game simple. For a slice of apple pie, you might suggest, "It's a tan triangle on the top and bottom." For an older child, you might say, "To make this dish, someone, somewhere, had to start off with a black oblong seed, and the seed had to grow into a tree."

If everyone in the group can read, you can limit the choices to items on the menu. The challenge comes from trying to mask the identity of the various dishes. For instance, spaghetti might be described as, "you can play pick-up sticks with it before you cook it—but not after."

As the game proceeds, no one will be guessing about where the food is—because it will be on the table before anyone knows it!

Wise Kids

Designer Coiffures

Here's how to keep your young child entertained in the hair salon while he or she is waiting for a cut—and perhaps plant the seeds for a career as a professional stylist!

Have your child invent wacky hairdos for men and women. Perhaps a great man's haircut would be shoulder-length on one side with three braids and two ponytails. As for color, bright purple would be the order of the day (a sight that might actually not be all that uncommon in some cities today!).

A woman's version might be longer, say down to the toes, incorporating five braids, and the hair would be dyed yellow and pink and tied with blue ribbons.

Alternatively, your child can create crazy coifs for animals. Perhaps long-hair cats would look elegant with pigtails, lions' manes should be plaited, and monkeys' tails should be decorated with banana slices. Just don't let your hairstylist try this at your salon!

What an Imagination!

Dino Palates

Anytime, Anyplace

Kids and dinosaurs—if kids had their way not only would dinosaurs still be around, but we would be keeping them as pets! But what would they eat!? Maybe your kids know the answer to that question. Read the dinosaurs from the list below and see if your dino experts know which ones are carnivores (C) and which are herbivores (H).

Tyrannosaurus Rex (C)
Centrosaurus (H)
Archaeopteryx (C)
Oviraptor (C)
Ankylosaurus (H)
Lesothosaurus (H)
Troödon (C)
Deinonychus (C)
Triceratops (H)
Allosaurus (C)
Protoceratops (H)
Coelophysis (C)
Megalosaurus (C)
Brachiosaurus (H)
Apatosaurus (H)
Dilophosaurus (C)
Diplodocus (H)
Albertosaurus (C)
Stegosaurus (H)
Velocirapter (C)

This game will get everyone's taste buds going—maybe for a side of palm leaves!

Dinosaur Safari

Anytime, Anyplace

Just imagine what it would be like for you and your kids to be teleported back in time to the days of the dinosaur. What do you think you would see?

If it sounds like a science fiction adventure, it is. But it's one that you can make up yourselves while waiting for traffic to move. Your car becomes a time-travel pod, and you and your children become chrononauts, traveling back to prehistoric times to research the terrible lizards.

To play, ask your kids to describe the cars and trucks as different dinosaurs. A crane might become a Brachiosaurus. That backhoe digging at the construction site could be a Maiasaur taking care of its young. A cement truck might become an armor-plated Stegosaurus.

Don't forget the rest of the prehistoric environment. Buildings can become fire-spewing volcanoes, while streetlights can do double duty as ferns.

You can modify this game to fit your child's interest. Turn your trip into an undersea adventure, for example. The fun will never dry up!

What an Imagination!

Doctor, Doctor

Anytime, Anyplace

Who says that we'll never find a cure for the common cold? In fact, your child just did, and all while the two of you were sitting in the waiting room!

This is too good a story to keep to yourself, so see whether your junior medical researcher will grant you an interview. Find out things like: How long he or she has been working on a cure for the common cold, how he or she stumbled onto the solution, what the cure involves, whether the cure will work for everyone, whether people will be able to cure themselves or will still need to go to doctors, whether we can dump all of the old cough syrups and throat lozenges or whether they'll still be useful, and so on.

Now that your child has discovered a cure for one of humankind's peskiest problems, what will he or she work on next? But first, see if your interviewee can take some time out to help you with a little medical problem you've been having for a couple of days—that annoying nose itch!

Reporter-at-Large

Door-to-Door Sales Pitches

Anytime, Anyplace

The days of the door-to-door vacuum cleaner salesperson may be over, but your child can revive their spirit by inventing "foot-in-the-door" openers for a variety of products, such as:

Vacuum Cleaners. Why not? "Aha, are you the man of the house? Why, I have just the thing to help you get rolling today!"

Major appliances. "I see that you have your breakfast all over your shirt. And our new model BX 240000 Super Washer is just the thing to get them out!"

Cars. In Japan, car salespeople actually do go door-to-door. So why not here? How about this line: "Your driveway is so wide it's just begging for another vehicle."

Toys. "I couldn't help noticing that your yard is too tidy and neat. What you clearly need here are some outdoor toys. No children? No problem! Play with them yourself and you'll feel ten years younger!"

Now then, can you sell your child on this game?

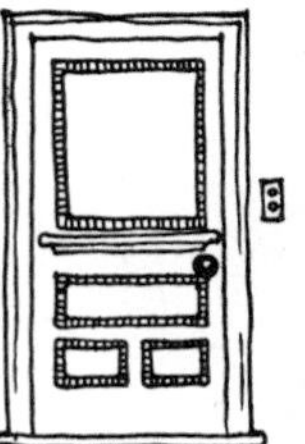

Easy Category Game

Anytime, Anyplace

Kids learn to sort and group objects at an early age. Here's how you can turn that basic skill into a game that makes time fly.

The easiest way to get started is to name two categories like hard and soft, then ask your kids to name as many objects as they can see that fit into those categories.

For variety, you can change the activity each time you play by selecting different categories: tall and short, or big and little, for example.

For older kids, you can bring their knowledge of everyday science into play with more abstract categories like hot and cold, or dry and wet. For the real science whizzes, see if they can find objects that fit into more than one category (water, for example—hard in the winter, soft in the summer).

The best thing about this game is that it can be played outside or indoors, proving the old adage, "a place for everything and everything in its place."

Observe the World

Events in History

How's your knowledge of history? It may never be the same after your children do this activity!

Anytime, Anyplace

Name some famous historical events and see what your kids can tell you about them. Perhaps you'd like to learn about the fall of the Roman Empire, the signing of the Declaration of Independence, or Captain Cook's visit to Hawaii.

For each event, ask your experts to name people, places, and dates. Don't worry if the answers aren't quite right; it will be interesting to learn what your kids know about history.

While you're learning about historical events, you might ask what life was like during the time periods in question. What did people wear? What kinds of jobs did they do? Did kids go to school, and if so, what did they learn? What did kids play with? And what was the most fun thing for children to do in those days?

Speaking of time, hopefully your kids are having so much fun that they aren't even noticing the minutes ticking away!

Everyday Heroes

There you are, stopped in traffic, waiting for that construction crane to move out of the way so you can get home and put supper on the table.

Suddenly, the crane starts to fall! Look out! This looks like a job for . . . Your Child!!!

You and your kids can construct dramatic rescues and feats of derring-do without ever leaving your car by using a little imagination and the scenery outside your window. Let your kids build a story of how they come to the aid of people in trouble; perhaps your kids will climb down that tall skyscraper with a hook and a rope to snare the falling crane.

Encourage your kids to play off their skills and interests. If they swim, maybe they can paddle out to the falling bridge and set it right. If they like the balance beam, maybe they can walk a tightrope between two buildings in order to save a cat caught at the very top.

This world could use some *real* heroes. Here's a chance for your kids to give it some.

What an Imagination!

Everything Machine

It's a clock, a can opener, a telephone, and a hair dryer—all in one!

Here's an opportunity to invent the ultimate combo machine and pass some waiting time.

Anytime, Anyplace

Ask your child to imagine a single machine that could do everything that we need to get done in a day, from the morning events to lights-out at night. The machine would have to be able to help with waking up, preparing breakfast, cleaning up dishes, whisking kids off to school and parents to work, meetings, errands, or back home again, picking kids up in the afternoon, preparing and serving meals at dinner time, getting everyone ready for bed, and finally making sure the house is closed up for the evening.

Have your child describe or draw the resulting contraption. Maybe it's a robot with wheels and seats. Or perhaps it's more like a car with mechanical arms. Whatever it is, we could sure use one at our house, so have your child send us a sketch immediately!

What an Imagination!

42 Family Award

Anytime, Anyplace

Which family on your block was recently nominated for the "Family of the Year" award? Why, yours, of course!

While you're waiting for the school bus to arrive, dinner to be ready, and so on, ask your child to explain why your family should win the award. Your child might cite a recent community or neighborhood effort, family outing, or a family project. Perhaps he or she will point to the colorful flower beds in front of your house as a great enhancement to the neighborhood.

You might also suggest that each family member has been nominated for a special, individual award. Your child can explain the award that family members have been nominated for and why they should win. Perhaps Mom is a great candidate for "Best Little League Coach," Dad is positioned to win the "Best Cookie Maker" award, and your child's younger brother is a potential "Best Teddy Bear Babysitter." Your child can even nominate him- or herself for an award: "Most Persuasive Orator of the Family!"

Fender-to-Fender Football

Here's a football activity that doesn't require any special equipment—or a ref, because there aren't any penalties.

Kick off the game by choosing offense or defense. The offensive player selects a color and tells it to the defensive player. To stop the offense from making a touchdown, the defensive player must find four objects (one per down) that are the same color as that named by the offense.

If the defense can't find the right-colored objects in a specified time, or before a specified distance is covered, the offense scores a first down. The offense gets to choose another color and attempts to make another first down. Two or three first downs take you all the way down the field for a touchdown, at which point offense and defense switch goals. If the defense does find four objects, the player becomes the offense.

To keep the game going, each player must choose a different (primary) color each time.

All right, sports fans, block the boredom—get off the sidelines and into the game!

Find the Shape

By
Appointment

There's not much to do in a doctor's office but look through old magazines or stare at the clock on the wall. But with this game, you can give your child a new way to look at his or her surroundings. Before you know it, the nurse will be calling you in.

To play, name a shape. If you're playing with a young child, stick with basic shapes like squares, circles, and triangles. After you name a shape, your child tries to find as many similar objects as he or she can. One rule: you have to play the whole game from your seat—no running around in the office.

For older kids, you can throw in some tougher shapes like diamonds, cylinders, spheres, and rectangles. You can even give combinations: find one sphere, two circles, and one square, for example. If that's too easy, pick one object from the room and give its shape, then see if your child can figure out what it is. Before you know it, you'll be teaching a geometry seminar right in the doctor's lobby!

Well, the doctor's always telling you to get in shape . . .

Observe the World

Flying Colors Meal

Waiting to Be Served

Here's an imagination game that will keep everyone's mind humming along while their food is simmering away in the restaurant kitchen.

The object is to see who can concoct a meal from the menu that would be entirely one color (or almost all one color). For instance, a green meal might consist of split pea soup, a salad with lettuce and avocados, a side order of green beans, and pistachio ice cream. A red meal might be tomato soup, tomato noodles with spaghetti sauce, red cabbage coleslaw, cranberry juice, and strawberry ice cream. Then try to come up with a white, purple, yellow, or orange meal.

First see who can make the meal as balanced and appealing as possible. Then suggest that everyone tries to make the zaniest meal possible, with odd concoctions and "exotic" foods.

Hmm, mashed potatoes covered with pink lemonade certainly would give you a pink vegetable. But you'll probably want to take a pass on it when it comes to ordering!

Food-Free Aisles

Shopping and Erranding

It seems like some supermarkets sell just about everything these days, and that food is the least of what they stock. See whether your child appreciates the range of what the local grocer offers.

When you begin your shopping, ask your child for a list of the non-food items the supermarket carries. He or she might cite such products as napkins, houseplants, and greeting cards. After your child has listed all the items he or she can think of, see whether the two of you can spot all the products as you walk up and down the aisles. Notice any non-food items your child may not have included, and see whether there are any surprises. Did you realize that your supermarket was selling the first book of a set of encyclopedias this week?

If you typically shop at a "super store," your child may find an extraordinary array of non-food items ranging from silverware to garden tools. Ask your child to point out the strangest "foods" your supermarket stocks. Isn't it amazing what passes for groceries these days?

Form Equals Function?

Walking There

You can't judge a building by its shape, but you and your kids can sure have fun using the building's form to guess what goes on inside!

If you're passing by a skyscraper, for example, ask your children what kinds of things the building might be used for. Maybe it's a great place to demonstrate parachutes or elevators (although the Otis Elevator company is actually housed in a one-story building!), assemble rockets, or test anti-gravity boots. Likewise, a long, low building might be the perfect place to make kite string or test giant rubber bands.

You can also expand the activity into a guessing game. Perhaps you've decided that a domed building would be a great place to raise a giant pumpkin. Give clues about farming, Halloween, pumpkin carving, and so on, or for an even greater challenge, convey your clues through charades.

Hmm, how about that fancy cylindrical building over there? Why, it's the perfect place to make giant peppermint patties!

What an Imagination!

48 Fresh off the Press

Shopping and Erranding

If your local supermarket offers weekly circulars, then you and your child have the makings of some appealing waiting games. Have your child pick up a circular at the store (or bring one from home), and ask him or her to find: all the fruits, the red items, the foods with seeds, the vegetables with leaves, and so on.

Your older child can use the circular to practice some supermarket math. You might ask, "What would it cost if we bought three jars of peanut butter and four cans of tuna?" Or, "If we had ten dollars, would we have enough money to buy a package of chicken, a bunch of broccoli, and two boxes of macaroni?"

Your kids can also match sale items from the circular with the real things on the shelves. If coupons are available, your children can be responsible for pointing them out to you. That may result in some unexpected purchases, though; you probably didn't expect to buy two jars of anchovy paste and get one free!

Garage Sale

Anytime, Anyplace

How would you like to plan a rainproof garage sale that's guaranteed to be a success? It's a great way to pass some time—profitably!

Simply point to the objects in your immediate surroundings, and have your child "sell" them to you. For example, let's say that you choose a clock on the wall. Your child can highlight all its selling points—its cool design, great timekeeping capabilities, comforting ticking sounds, and so on—and then, if you're interested in buying it, make an offer and begin the bartering process.

Once your child gets the hang of it, let him or her establish a price for each object in sight, no matter how big or small (yes, the Brooklyn Bridge is up for sale, as are those small pebbles on the sidewalk and the paper clips on the receptionist's desk). Can the two of you come to an agreement on all of the "merchandise" in view? Maybe you can even work out a package deal—as long as you promise to take immediate possession of the goods!

Curtain Call

Geo Wizards

Anytime, Anyplace

Does your child enjoy talking about places he or she has visited, or might someday like to visit? If so, this is a great game to play when you have a few minutes to spare.

Start off with a state or country that your family has been to during a trip or a visit to a relative's or friend's home. Then ask your child to provide a description of the place that includes the climate, terrain, history, unique plants and animals, unusual foods, special landmarks, natural wonders, and other details that capture the essence of the area.

Now try the same with places that your child hasn't actually visited, but has learned about through books, classroom studies, or videos. Pick a location that you have some knowledge of, so you can prompt for descriptions and key facts.

Still need to pass some time? Then ask your child to describe an imaginary place, perhaps from a book he or she has read, or a place that's pure fantasy.

One thing is certain; wherever you and your child "travel" today, you're bound to learn some exciting new facts!

Geo Word Game

Anytime, Anyplace

Here's a fun word game that uses the names of places. It doesn't take more than a good memory for geography, but watch out—the longer you play, the harder it gets.

The rules are simple. One player starts by saying the name of a place—town, city, state, country, and so on. Each player in turn has to think of a place name that begins with the *last* letter of the previous place.

For example, the first player might start with "New York." Player two could say "Kansas," leaving player three with an *S*. The game could then go on with Saskatoon, Nepal, Loui-siana, Amarillo, Oregon, New Hampshire, Ethiopia, Arkansas, Santa Barbara, Anchorage—until a player gets stumped!

If your kids have fun with this game, you can try it with other categories as well, like foods or people's names. No doubt, the waiting time will be over long before you've run out of words to use!

Ghost Runners

Gridlock Busters

All right, sports fans, here's a fast-moving activity that makes time move faster than an Olympic sprinter in the fifty-yard dash.

This play race works best downtown, or anyplace where there's a lot of action on the street. To set up the game, each player imagines a ghost runner who must get from one end of the street to the other. When you shout, "Go!," you and your kids talk your runners along the "track."

The comments from the "fans" (you and your kids) are what make this game so much fun. "My guy will have to avoid that newsstand if he wants to maintain his lead," you might say. Your kids might counter with "Whoa, look at the way Betty swerved to get away from that revolving door! I don't believe it—she hopped onto the awning in front of the stereo shop and used it as a trampoline to spring herself into the lead!"

You never know—this might be all the preparation your kid needs to land a job as a major league sportscaster!

Curtain Call

Great Answering Machine Tapes

Anytime, Anyplace

"This is the Smith's house. Please leave a message and we'll call you back later." Oh, yawn. Your kids can no doubt improve on that answering machine message and have some waiting time fun in the process. Let them devise some messages about:

Famous people. How about, "Hi, this is Ben Franklin, I'm out flying a kite in a lightning storm and can't talk to you now. Catch you later. Ahhhhhhhhhh!"

Zany Situations. Perhaps, "Hi. This is George, I can't talk now because I'm hanging upside down from the tree in the backyard doing my homework!"

Silly Voice Mail Menus. Take revenge on today's awful voice mail systems with something like: "Hi. Press one if you want to leave a message, then choose from the following thirty-two choices, spin twice, touch your ear, hang up, and send us a letter!"

Leave any waiting grumpies at the beep!

Curtain Call

Guess That Creature

Anytime, Anyplace

Hey, is that a real flamingo over in the corner, or is it just your child playacting?

Choose a creature (mammal, fish, bird, or insect), and have your child improvise a member of the species. He or she acts out the creature physically (by hopping, leaping, flapping his or her "wings," standing on one leg, and so on). Your job is to guess which type of creature your child is playacting.

If you need additional clues, your child might turn his or her creature into a talking animal, fish, bird, or insect, and offer clues. A flying fish, for example, might say something like, "I mainly live in the water, but I enjoy taking to the air now and then." A caterpillar might say, "It takes a long time for me to tie my eighteen shoes . . . but after sleeping for a while, I'll wake up and only have to worry about six—when I'm not flying, that is."

Once you guess your child's creature, you can improvise another and see if your child can figure out what you are. Don't worry about anyone staring—it's all in a day's wait!

Habitats

Anytime, Anyplace

Your kids might be able to tell you that giraffes live in Africa and that polar bears live where it's cold. But could they tell what part of the world (rain forests, mountains, or grasslands) some really unusual animals, like the following, live in? Find out and pass some time while you're at it!

Harpy Eagle (Rain forests) • Lesser Panda (Mountains) • Snow Leopard (Mountains) • Puff Adder (a snake—Grasslands) • Kinkajou (a tree-dwelling mammal—Rain forests) • Paca (a small mammal—Rain forests) • Gnu (another name for Wildebeest—Grasslands) • Great Potoo (bird—Rain forests) • Eland (large antelope—Grasslands) • Weaver Birds (Grasslands) • Caiman (relative of crocodile—Rain forests) • Pika (tiny mammal—Mountains) • Dung Beetles (Grasslands) • Capybara (largest rodent in world—Rain forests) • Chinchilla (tiny mammal—Mountains) • Secretary Bird (Grasslands) • Purple Honeycreeper (colorful bird—Rain forests) • Banded Mongoose (predatory mammal—Grasslands) • Coati (relative of raccoon—Rain forests) • Barbary Sheep (Mountains)

The Cassowary

Now then, how about a trip to the natural history museum or zoo to actually see some of these critters!

Hand Signals

Why should people who drive cars using hand signals have all the fun? Your child can use a similar body language to direct you while you're walking to an appointment or event.

Have your child develop hand signals that designate a left turn, right turn, straight ahead motion, or reverse motion. Then let your child direct you, using those signs to let you and other followers know what to do (of course, when your child reaches the end of a street or the corner, he or she should adhere to your family's standard safety rules and let you take over the position of leader as necessary).

Enhance the language by developing additional signals. For example, raising the left arm twice might mean "hop on your right foot until further notice," making the victory sign with the left hand might mean "take baby steps," and raising both arms at once might mean "step over cracks in the sidewalk."

See how long you can follow your child's hand signals before you get confused!

Head in the Sand

Anytime, Anyplace

How would your child like to interview some people who just saw an ostrich escape from a zoo—or even the ostrich itself?

Play the part of a reporter and interview your child, who pretends to be an eyewitness at the zoo when an ostrich escaped. Ask the eyewitness such questions as: How did the ostrich escape? Which direction was the ostrich headed in when you last saw it? Did the ostrich have any food or belongings with it? How would people be able to recognize this ostrich if they ran into it? Did the ostrich appear to be healthy? And so on.

Then shift gears, and your child can play the part of the escaped ostrich. Ask the ostrich why he or she escaped, how the ostrich will find food and shelter while on the road, what the ostrich's ultimate destination is, whether he or she intends to get in contact with any zoo friends eventually, and the like.

One thing you and your child can prove—waiting time doesn't have to get zooey!

Reporter-at-Large

Historical Interview

Anytime, Anyplace

Wouldn't it be neat to ask George Washington what it was like to cross the Delaware? Or what Isaac Newton felt when the apple fell on his head and he discovered gravity? Well you can, with this waiting game!

Have your child select a figure from history—a great leader, inventor/scientist, artist, writer, and so on. Then take turns role-playing the interviewee and the interviewer, asking questions about:

The life and times. What was life back then like? What did people eat and wear? Was it fun to live back then?

The interviewee's life. What was your family like? What was your favorite thing to do? What's your fondest memory? Worst memory? Greatest challenge?

Key events. What was it like when you [crossed the river, made the discovery, and so forth]? What would you do differently if you could do it all over?

Wow, Mr. Newton, we didn't realize that apple seeds got into your ears and took a whole week to retrieve!

Reporter-at-Large

Historical Tour

How would you like to tour a museum while you're waiting? Well, get ready to have your child take you on an instant tour of the Anywhere Museum!

Anytime, Anyplace

Your child can lead you on a guided walk through an office building, the subway stop, or wherever you happen to be, pointing out all of the original features (such as the stairway that was handcarved by the first carpenter in Neanderthal times), the newer additions (like the drinking fountain that was installed just after the discovery of metal), interesting furnishings (such as the chair that George Washington sat in when he came to town), and so on.

In addition, your tour guide/child can tell you about previous occupants of the house or building: their names, occupations, favorite pastimes, any additions or modifications that they made to the structure, and so on. Be sure to ask lots of questions of your guide—everything in the museum probably has a fascinating hidden history!

How Many Words?

Waiting to Be Served

What's in a restaurant's name and a restaurant's menu? Good waiting games for your kids, probably.

First try seeing how many distinct words your children can discover using the letters in the name of the restaurant you're patronizing. If the establishment is called something like "The Grand Old New England Clam Chowder House," it'll be easy for everyone to come up with a slew of words. If it's "Al's," you might want to try using words from the menu. For instance, how many words can people find in sandwich entrees such as "Hamburger Deluxe" or "Grilled Cheese Special?" Make sure each player gets a chance to pick a section of the menu for the next round of the game.

As a variation, each player tries to find his or her name in the fewest number of words on the menu. To make the name "Steve," for example, you'd need a "Side Order," (an "s" and two "e's"), a "Taco" (for the "t"), and "Virginia Ham" (for the "v").

As these games will show, it pays to go to restaurants with varied menus!

Word Wizards

How to . . .

Anytime, Anyplace

We all take for granted the simple things in life, like tying our shoes or brushing our teeth. As your child will find, explaining the "little things" in life is actually far more difficult than it sounds. And it's a great way to pass the time, too.

Ask your child to serve as a "human instruction manual" who provides step-by-step instructions for common actions such as double knotting shoelaces, folding a napkin, peddling a bicycle, making a bed, scratching an itch on your back, and so on.

Once your child gets the hang of it, ask him or her to explain the techniques for assembling a block or Lego castle, folding a paper airplane, or making the perfect mudpie.

And for the ultimate challenge, see if your child can explain how to talk, sing, dance, read, or perform addition and subtraction. Maybe he or she will have some insights into describing an incredibly useful, but often lost, skill: listening!

How to Be Brave

By Appointment

It's bad enough when your child has to sit in a doctor's waiting room for a long time; it's worse when he or she dreads the appointment. Here's a way to make the time pass more quickly and dispel some anxiety.

Do a little role reversal, and have your child ask you various questions, such as, "So what's the doctor going to do today?" You then talk about what's likely to happen and ask your child what you can do to be brave.

You can also provide some comic relief by offering silly scenarios, such as, "Well, I'm a bit nervous, because the doctor is going to put Oreo cookies between my toes and stinky cheese on my head." Your child can then assure you that there's nothing to worry about; the cheese aroma won't last more than a month, and the cookie filling will keep your feet warm during winter!

When it's time to see the doctor, your child will be giggling with a host of remedies to share with the medical staff!

What an Imagination!

Howdy, Neighbor

63

Anytime, Anyplace

Here's a quick quiz to challenge your children's knowledge of U.S. geography. In the list below, the first state in each set shares a border with some or all of the other states in that set. Can your kids tell you which ones share borders? (Correct answers are in *italics.*)

Wyoming shares a border with—North Dakota? *South Dakota?*
Maryland shares a border with—*Delaware? West Virginia?* New Jersey?
New Mexico shares a border with—*Oklahoma?* Nevada?
Vermont shares a border with—Maine? *New Hampshire? Massachusetts?*
Kansas shares a border with—Arkansas? *Colorado? Missouri?*
South Carolina shares a border with—Florida? *Georgia?* Tennessee?
California shares a border with—Idaho? *Arizona? Nevada?*
Wisconsin shares a border with—*Michigan? Iowa?* Indiana?
Texas shares a border with—*New Mexico? Oklahoma? Arkansas? Louisiana?*

And for a bonus, ask: The Mississippi River runs along or through ten states—What are they? *(Minnesota, Wisconsin, Iowa, Illinois, Missouri, Kentucky, Tennessee, Arkansas, Mississippi, and Louisiana.)*

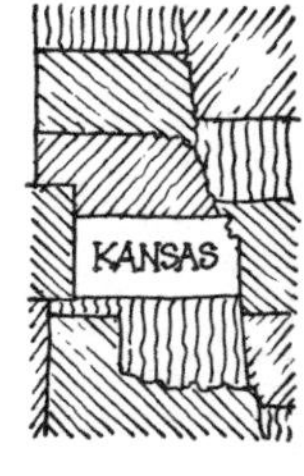

Humdinger

Anytime, Anyplace

Making music is one of the best ways we have of passing the time. Here are some suggestions for using singing to create your own waiting games.

If you have young kids with you, take turns humming a song and see who can guess the name. Stick to old favorites like "This Old Man." During special holidays, try humming seasonal tunes.

Another musical game—"song charades"—doesn't involve humming or singing at all. One player silently acts out a song, while the others try to guess what it is. An alternative way to guess is to hum the tune instead of saying the answer.

Other variations include clapping out a tune, and humming a song in a monotone.

Finally, do a "Johnny-One-Note" hum-along. To play, choose a song. Each person hums a single note in turn, around and around until the whole song is sung. Kind of makes you feel like you're part of a human pipe organ!

If the Walls Could Talk

Release your child's imagination with this story activity that gives a voice to the inanimate objects all around you. Take the old bank there on the corner. What's it thinking? What does it sound like? If it could talk, what would it say?

In this activity, you and your child take turns speaking like the cars, trucks, buildings, signs, and structures that surround your car during rush hour. If your child doesn't know how to begin, start with something like the Walk/Don't Walk light at the intersection. " 'Please be careful,' says the light," you might say. " 'Look both ways. Hurry across now.' "

Movie theaters are always great conversationalists. "Come right on in," they say from their big dark doorways. "It's a really great show I've got playing here."

The vehicles on the road in front and to the side can provide a lot of fun as they jostle for position. "Excuse me," says the taxi cab, pushing its nose in front of the bus. "Well, I never," exclaims the bus. "The nerve!"

What an Imagination!

Instant Grown-ups

Anytime, Anyplace

What if your children woke up one morning to find that they had suddenly acquired adult bodies? Ask how they would:

Explain to their friends and family members who they were. How would your kids convince everyone that they were still the same people?

Handle school. Would your kids still go to school if they didn't look like children? How would being a student be different if they didn't look like the rest of the kids?

Take advantage of their size. How would their new bodies affect their ability to play on team sports? Would they have to play with one hand tied behind their back? How would they sit in a cafeteria scaled down for kids?

Once your children have thought about what it might be like to be a child in an adult's body, pose this question: If you could have an adult body overnight, would you want to?

Intergalactic Interview

Anytime, Anyplace

Wouldn't you like to interview an astronaut while you're waiting? Well, designate your child an intergalactic traveler, and see whether you can snag a one-on-one conversation.

Your child role-plays a space traveler who has just returned from an intergalactic mission. As the first reporter on the scene, your job is to get all the information you can about the expedition. Ask such questions as: Which planets did you visit? How long did you spend in outer space? What did you do to pass the time while you were traveling? Did you meet any life forms on other planets? What did you find on the most interesting planets you visited? How did the moons you visited differ from our moon? What did you eat while you were traveling?

Perhaps your child brought some surprises back to earth, like some otherworldly rocks, seashells, instant pictures, plants—or even a new alien buddy. See whether you can be the first earthling reporter to get an interview with an extraterrestrial once you've finished interviewing your child!

Reporter-at-Large

Invisible Kids

Anytime, Anyplace

What if your children were suddenly *heard but not seen* because they were invisible? Ask how they would:

Enjoy the perks of being invisible. What would your kids do that visible kids can't? Would they still take baths? Would they get sneak previews of museum exhibits off-limits to the public?

Conduct themselves in public. What pleasant mischief would they get themselves into? Perhaps they'd tickle people waiting in line in stores or adjust people's hats as they rode a bus.

Get people's attention politely and without scaring them. If your kids sat down, how would they let people know "this seat is taken?" How would your children let teachers know when they wanted to be called on? How would your kids greet their friends and initiate conversations?

Once your kids have thought about what it might be like to be invisible, pose this question: If you could be heard but not seen, would you?

Item Counter

Shopping and Erranding

Don't you wish people with a shopping cart full of items would learn to *not* stand in the supermarket's express check-out line? Well, perhaps if they had your child to help them take an item count from time to time they would be more concious of the item limit.

You can keep a handle on how many goods you have in your cart at any given moment by assigning your child the role of official item-counter. If your goal is to find out whether or not you can stand in an express line, your child can keep you on your toes by sounding an alert when you're about to reach that line's quota.

Of course, if yours is the type of shopping trip our family usually makes, your goal might be less lofty: just let your kid have some fun! To that end, encourage your kids to take license in their counting, and you can see whether your count matches theirs. Now, do you count a dozen eggs as *one* box or *twelve* eggs?

Just Hangin' Around

Anytime, Anyplace

A new world's record for hang gliding has just been set: a pilot has floated aloft for three weeks. Now's your chance, as reporter-at-large, to interview the record setter. Here are some questions to ask: What kind of exercises did you do to keep from getting stiff? How did you sleep? What did you do to keep from getting bored? Was it scary during thunderstorms? Did birds bother you? Did anyone wave at you from airplanes? What was the best part of your excursion? Would you do it again?

Next, ask the pilot for his or her plans for the future, and what other hang gliding events he or she would like to set records in. Also ask what he or she missed the most while in the air—maybe a nice firm mattress and box spring.

Finally, how about asking this one: Did any Canadian geese invite you to join their formation?

Reporter-at-Large

Kid Pix

By Appointment

Most pediatricians' offices have lots of pictures of children—photographs of patients, or drawings and photos in brochures, pamphlets, magazines, posters, and paintings. Here's how you can use them while you wait your turn for your child to be seen.

First see how many pictures of kids your child can find. If your child hasn't developed counting skills yet, he or she can simply point to each picture and you can keep a running tally. Next, have your junior sleuth track down all the pictures of babies, all those of girls, all the boys, and so on.

If the wait is really dragging on, you can suggest various "specialty" hunts, such as all the girls with brown hair, all the boys with glasses, everyone wearing something red, everyone smiling, and so on.

If you have more than one child with you, each can be assigned a certain type of picture to find. You can up the challenge by limiting the time of the picture hunt.

Hey, there's a fun-looking family—it's yours!

Observe the World

Kids' Book of Home Remedies

Anytime, Anyplace

So you have the hiccups? Ask your resident experts what to do. And pass some waiting time in the process, too.

The object of this activity is to see how creative your child can be when it comes to solving some of life's pesky little problems, like hiccups. Perhaps the cure lies in covering your ears while you try to spell the titles of your favorite ice-cream flavors—backwards. For that matter, maybe the only solution is to have some ice cream!

Ask about all sorts of "conditions," such as what to do when you have: drunk a soda too quickly, consumed something with too much pepper, exhausted your ear from talking on the phone too long, tired out your cheeks from smiling too much, gotten a sore tummy from laughing too hard, acquired an itch in the middle of your back that refuses to go away, or charged up your hair with static electricity.

Now here's one for your problem solver—what to do about those eyeglasses that keep slipping down your nose!

What an Imagination!

Know Your Postal Codes

Anytime, Anyplace

How well do your kids know U.S. geography? Put them to the test by having them try to name all fifty states! Then see if your children can tell you the abbreviation for each state—or tell your kids an abbreviation and have them identify the state.

Alabama	AL	Montana	MT
Alaska	AK	Nebraska	NE
Arizona	AZ	Nevada	NV
Arkansas	AR	New Hampshire	NH
California	CA	New Jersey	NJ
Colorado	CO	New Mexico	NM
Connecticut	CT	New York	NY
Delaware	DE	North Carolina	NC
Florida	FL	North Dakota	ND
Georgia	GA	Ohio	OH
Hawaii	HI	Oklahoma	OK
Idaho	ID	Oregon	OR
Illinois	IL	Pennsylvania	PA
Indiana	IN	Rhode Island	RI
Iowa	IA	South Carolina	SC
Kansas	KS	South Dakota	SD
Kentucky	KY	Tennessee	TN
Louisiana	LA	Texas	TX
Maine	ME	Utah	UT
Maryland	MD	Vermont	VT
Massachusetts	MA	Virginia	VA
Michigan	MI	Washington	WA
Minnesota	MN	West Virginia	WV
Mississippi	MS	Wisconsin	WI
Missouri	MO	Wyoming	WY

Bonus question: who knows their nine-digit zip code? Beats us!

Wise Kids

Know Your Vitamins

Anytime, Anyplace

Your children have probably heard about the importance of vitamins. But do they know what the various vitamins do and where they can be found (other than in a pill)? Try this activity and find out. First ask why we need the following vitamins, among others.

Vitamin A (Maintains healthy skin and hair, aids in night vision) • Vitamin B12 (Helps in building red blood cells and in keeping the nervous system working properly) • Vitamin C (Builds strong gums, teeth, connective tissue, and bones) • Vitamin D (Builds strong bones and teeth) • Vitamin E (Aids in the formation of red blood cells and muscles) • Vitamin K (Helps blood to clot)

Next, ask what foods contain various vitamins. Either list a food and see who can identify the corresponding vitamin, or rattle off the vitamins and see who knows the associated food.

Carrots, broccoli, spinach, cantaloupe—Vitamin A • Meat, fish, eggs, milk—Vitamin B_{12} • Citrus fruits, tomatoes, potatoes—Vitamin C • Milk—Vitamin D • Vegetables, whole-grain cereals and bread—Vitamin E • Leafy green vegetables, peas, potatoes—Vitamin K

The next time you plan a meal, you might want to consult your junior nutrition expert about eating right!

Landmark Locations

Here's a fun and easy way to pass the time. See if your children can name the locations of the famous landmarks on this list.

Anytime, Anyplace

Statue of Liberty—New York City, NY
Golden Gate Bridge—San Francisco, CA
Eiffel Tower—Paris, France
Pyramids—Egypt
Taj Mahal—India
Lincoln Memorial—Washington, DC
Everglades—Florida
Giant Redwoods—California
Sears Tower—Chicago, IL
Niagara Falls—New York and Canada
Grand Canyon—Arizona
Gateway Arch—St. Louis, MO
Great Barrier Reef—Australia
London Bridge—Lake Havasu City, AZ
(really, it is!)
United Nations—New York City, NY
Dead Sea—Israel and Jordan
Panama Canal—Panama
Old Faithful—Yellowstone National Park, WY
Mt. Rushmore—South Dakota
The Great Wall—China
Leaning Tower of Pisa—Pisa, Italy

For a twist, try tossing in a few not-so-famous places that your family has visited. Where is Aunt Shirlee's house, anyway?

76 Landscape Architects

Do you see that bed of tulips, over by the red maple trees and fountain, beside your neighbor's garage? Well, with a bit of imagination, you and your child can!

The next time you and your children have to walk somewhere, designate someone as "landscape architect." He or she now has the magical power to beautify or redecorate the neighborhood by planting imaginary trees, shrubs, and flowers, and constructing benches, sculptures, and fountains anyplace—just by thinking it.

Encourage your child to share his or her vision with you. Ask about the changes he or she would make to the landscape, the longer-term improvements, how the changes would be accomplished, what the new colors and designs would be, and so on. This could be the start of great improvements to the neighborhood—and the seeds of a brilliant career for your child!

Letter Starters

Need a fast, short, easy game to play with your kids? This game turns any wait into a red-letter day.

Anytime, Anyplace

Start the game by naming a letter. Then, on the simplest level, your child must list as many things beginning with that letter as he or she can see in the immediate surroundings. If more than one child is playing, each child should take a turn naming an object. To increase the challenge, ask your kids to name objects that end with the letter you have selected.

A variation involves entire words. To play, name the word: "hat," for example. The key here is to keep the words simple—no more than three or four letters. Your kids must find three objects, each of which contains one letter of the selected word—like "helicopter," "animal," and "lamppost." Modify the difficulty level by letting kids use any letters in the objects they see, or by restricting them to beginning or ending letters.

Here's a chance for any child to earn his or her letter jacket while you wait!

Wise Kids

Life Without Laws

Anytime.
Anyplace

What if we woke up and our society was without laws, and it was up to individuals to rebuild our laws from scratch? Ask your kids how they would:

Decide for themselves what's right and wrong. How could they be certain that their choices were the best ones? How would they determine what's fair?

Get people to agree to behave in ways that benefit everyone. What if everyone felt differently about certain issues, like speed limits? Could your kids convince drivers to slow down when they approached a school or a neighborhood?

Preserve order at home and in the community. Who would enforce the new laws?

Once your kids have thought about what it might be like to live in a law-free society, pose this question: Would you like to live in a world without laws and rules?

Lights Out

Anytime, Anyplace

What if electricity were "uninvented," and there were no other power sources? Ask your kids how they would:

Entertain themselves. If televisions, radios, VCR's, and computers didn't work, what would your kids do for fun?

Keep warm in the winter and cool in the summertime. How could your kids survive the winter and summer without heaters, fans, or air conditioners?

Adjust their diets. Without conventional or microwave ovens, what foods would be difficult to prepare? Would your kids find other ways to cook, or would they eat other things instead?

Take advantage of the situation. What would the benefits of having no electricity be to people? What would the benefits to the environment be?

Once your kids have thought about what it might be like to live in a world with no electricity, ask: Would you pull the plug on electricity, even for a short period of time, if it were up to you?

80 Like Night and Day

Walking There

If you're walking to an appointment or going to an event with your younger child, here's a great game you can play. It's guaranteed to make you notice how interesting every block can be.

Ask your child to point out all the contrasts he or she can find as you're walking. You might suggest the categories: big and small, light and heavy, rough and smooth, loud and soft, narrow and wide, tall and short, and so on. See how many pairs you and your child can think of together in each category. Alternatively, your child can give you some pairs, and your job is to figure out the category (for instance, caterpillar and ant, and steamroller and motorcycle might be examples of "slow and fast").

You and your child might also want to single out interesting pairs of objects, and see how many contrasts you can think of that fit them. For instance, a dog and cat might be "shaggy and smooth," "spotted and solid," "talkative and quiet," "friendly and shy," or even "big barker and small meower"!

Line Math

Waiting in Line

When are we going to get our tickets? When is it our turn? You can offer some precise answers after you and your older children do some "line math."

Try computing how fast the line is moving by picking something on the floor or ground that will serve as a marker, then timing how long it takes to move, say, three feet (approximate as best you can). Take a best guess as to how far you are from the beginning of the line, and have your child calculate how long it will take to "get there." (Having a pad and pencil will help.)

Another way to compute the time is observe how many people are admitted, purchase tickets, or whatever, every minute, then count how many people are in front of you. Some quick math will give you a precise answer.

What to do if the waiting seems awfully long? Why, see who can convert the waiting times into fractions of a day, week, month, year, decade, or century. See, it's not such a long time after all!

82 Line Races

Shopping and Erranding

Isn't it about time you learned to pick the fastest checkout line at the supermarket? Perhaps, with the help of your child's keen eye for detail, you can.

Ask your child to predict which line will move the fastest and explain why. Perhaps the express line, which is the longest, is still the best bet because customers have the fewest purchases. Or maybe the cashier in aisle six has the shortest line, and is working at warp speed, so her line is sure to move the most quickly. You might choose the line your child recommends, or pick another as a "control" and see whether or not your child was right.

Your child can also officiate at a "Line Olympics." While you're waiting in line, your child can keep an eye on two different lines (the ones on either side of yours), and predict which line will move the fastest. The easiest method is to keep an eye on customers in specific positions (say, the fourth person in line), and see which ones pay for their purchases first.

Hmm, do you think that couple with four grocery carts will ever get through the line?

Lion's Paws and Gaping Maws

By Appointment

Hey, what's that lion doing here in the doctor's waiting room? Probably waiting to have a thorn pulled out of his paw.

As you wait your turn with the doctor, ask your child to imagine how he or she would treat a lion (or any other animal) with an injured paw. Young children can even demonstrate proper medical techniques with a stuffed animal, if the waiting room has one, or by using your hand (perhaps thorn removal requires applying pressure in just the right way—with a strong chin). Be sure to have your child offer the lion words of consolation and advice on how to be brave.

Suggest other scenarios as well, such as an elephant whose trunk became clogged with peanuts (the doctor always keeps a special vacuum attachment for such problems), or the hippo whose mouth got stuck open when she yawned too wide (tickling behind the ears is a proven method for such problems!).

Now then, how will your child treat that poor octopus with the sucker that seems permanently stuck to a Ping-Pong ball?

What an Imagination!

Make a Meal

Shopping and Erranding

Your child probably has a pretty good idea of what you're going to do with the food in your shopping cart. But what could he or she create with the ingredients in the *other* carts in front or in back of yours in the checkout line?

As you wend your way toward the cash register, have your child describe various dishes that could be made from the foods others are buying. The dishes can be real or silly—a pack of ground beef and buns would be a good indication that barbecue fare is in order. But there's no reason why it couldn't be combined with one of the cereals to make Beef Crispies—the perfect food for people who work nights and aren't quite ready for breakfast when they get home.

Your child can also describe the various steps that he or she would use to prepare the food—sautéing, mixing, blending, or for that matter, stomping, sitting on, tossing.

Oh, dear—what will he or she do with the dog food and toothpaste?

What an Imagination!

Make an Acronym

Know what "WAIT" stands for? "We're An Incredible Team." What other acronyms can you and your kids devise while you're waiting?

Anytime, Anyplace

First, explain to your children that acronyms are words formed from the first letters or parts of other words, such as "RADAR" (which stands for "*RA*dio *D*etecting *A*nd *R*anging"). Then see how many acronyms your kids can devise for various categories, such as dinosaurs ("TROLL": T-Rex On Left Lamppost); animals ("TAG": Turtles Are Great); or silly stuff ("WALT": We All Love Tweezers). Then see if people can guess what the acronyms mean based on charades.

Players can also use their names as acronyms and describe what they stand for. The name "Noah," for instance, could be the acronym for "Nation Of Apple Harvesters."

Now, what will you do if your name is Bartholomew?

Mechanical Advantage

Anytime, Anyplace

What if machine-powered travel didn't exist? Ask your kids how they would:

Get around. What vehicles would still work? (bicycles, sailboats, gliders, hot-air balloons, in-line skates, and so on)? Would engineless modes of transportation be more or less pleasant than the powered means of transit? Which places would it be most difficult to get to?

Decide when to take long trips. How would vacations be different if traveling were so much slower and less comfortable?

Learn about the world. How might things change if people from different continents rarely got a chance to meet one another?

Once your kids have thought about life without modern means of transportation, pose this question: Would you prefer it if there were no powered engines in the world?

Meet the Olympiad

If you've always wanted to meet a world-famous Olympic champion, here's your chance. Your child role-plays a sports star fresh from the Zany Olympics, and you conduct an exclusive interview while you're waiting.

Anytime, Anyplace

Ask such questions as: Where were the Zany Olympics held? What did you think of your competitors and teammates? Which event did you participate in? How did you train? What were the biggest challenges on your road to becoming a world-renowned Olympiad? What does your Olympic medal look like? and so on.

Then find out what your child learned while participating in the Zany Olympics. What are the benefits of having athletes from different parts of the globe getting together? What's it like to represent your country in front of the rest of the world? How did audience members respond to the athletes' accomplishments? Perhaps your child can also explain the longest-lasting benefit of being the world's gold medal-winning grape-tosser!

Reporter-at-Large

Menu Math

Waiting to Be Served

You've probably heard stories about someone who walked into a restaurant and ordered one of everything on the menu. What would that maneuver cost in the restaurant you're patronizing? Let your junior math whizzes determine that for you—and you won't have to worry about consuming all those calories!

Ask your kids who can sum up all of the items on the menu, including all possible options, such as toppings and "extras." For an added kicker, see if they can determine the sales and/or meal tax.

A variation on the activity is to have your child convert the menu prices into coinage ($4.65 could be sixteen quarters, four dimes, four nickels, and five pennies). Older kids can also break down the menu by food type, say, totaling everything with meat in it, everything made with dairy products or tomato sauce, and so on.

Finally, have one of your whiz kids imagine that he or she is the waitperson attending your table—what kind of tip would be in order?

Menu Word Games

Waiting to Be Served

A menu is more than just a passport to satisfied tummies; it can be a ticket to word fun and games that take the edge off waiting for your order to be taken or your food to arrive.

One simple menu game that will appeal to young readers involves word clues. You might say something like, "I'm looking at a word that begins with *m* and ends with *k*, and has four letters." The first player to find "milk" gets to select a word for the next round.

For an older child, you can make the clues more challenging. You might give the clue for the *m* in milk as "the eighth letter alphabetically after the first letter of the name of an animal who would be most helpful if our shower broke" (an elephant). For the *k*, the clue might be something like, "the last letter sometimes sounds like another letter in our alphabet that in turn sounds like something that you do with your eyes ('see—i.e. *c*)." Finally, for the number of letters, offer a clue that requires some addition, subtraction, or whatever mathematical operations the players can do. What an equation for fun!

Word Wizards

Modern Conveniences

Anytime, Anyplace

So your kids are tired of waiting and are getting bored? Just have them look around at all the exciting things that have interesting histories.

Take that doorknob over there. Who invented it? And when? Ask your resident expert questions like "Why were doorknobs necessary?" "What did people do without them?" "What was the person's name who came up with the idea?" "What kind of commotion did the invention make in the town where the inventor lived?" and so on.

You can also turn the session into a role-play activity, during which you take the position of a naysayer. "What? Impossible! Doorknobs will forever alter the shape of human hands!!!"

You can play this game with just about anything from concrete and glass to shoelaces and ballpoint pens. All of the things you take for granted are grist for the expert's mill. For that matter, what *is* the story behind the old gristmill?

Month, Please

Sure, everyone knows that most holidays come but once a year. But does your child know in which months they take place?

Anytime, Anyplace

Name a holiday, or another special day or event (such as a family member's birthday, the first day of school, the week when you'll be visiting a relative's house, and so on), and see whether your child can tell you in which month it's slated to happen. Older "wise kids" might tell you the exact days as well as the months—for example, your child might know that Thanksgiving falls on the fourth Thursday in November, Groundhog Day is February 2, and New Year's Eve occurs on December 31.

The better your child gets at this game, the more challenging you can make your questions. For the wisest kids (and adults), you might ask for the date of the summer solstice (about June 22), the first day of autumn (around September 23), or even when daylight savings time begins!

More Coin Games

Anytime, Anyplace

What are coins really worth these days? Ask your child to answer that question without looking at the money, and you'll find the time flying.

Have your child close his or her eyes, then place a quarter, dime, nickel, and penny in his or her hand. See if he or she can identify which is which. If your child can't feel the difference between the coins, give him or her an "eyes open study period" first. For hotshots, try including a "ringer," say two pennies and no dime—will your child recognize the trick or convince him- or herself that one of the pennies is actually a dime?

As a variation, see if your child can find a dollar's worth of coins, five coins that add up to forty-five cents, or five coins that add up to nine cents—all with his or her eyes closed.

Hey, how about this one: how many quarters will it take to pay the parking ticket that the meter maid is about to tuck under your windshield?

Most Important Numbers

Anytime, Anyplace

Of course, every child *knows* his or her birthday. But can your kids *find* the date by looking at the numbers on signs, clocks, magazines, and so on?

Have your children translate their birthdays into numerical form, including the month, day, and year (for example, 6-10-87 and 3-31-90). Then see if they can find those numbers, in sequence, as you walk or ride (check house, road, and exit numbers), or while you sit (look at magazines and newspapers, or a calendar).

Once your kids find their birthdays, see whether they can find yours and other family members'. Then have them look for other familiar dates, with or without years, such as 7-4 (Independence Day), 2-14 (Valentine's Day), and so on. Your child can also seek other important, non-date numbers, such as telephone numbers, addresses, ages, and so on.

Can anybody find his or her social security number—all in one source?

Mosts and Leasts

Waiting in Line

Do you feel like you've blended into a homogeneous line, a veritable mass of humanity? With a little observation on your child's part, the line will suddenly take on a unique life of its own.

Have your child look at the people in line and observe the following (noting the most and least common): clothing colors in general (clothing, purses, bags), as well the colors of specific apparel, such as hats, coats, pants, etc; hair color—men, women, and everyone in line; clothing styles (for example, how many people have shorts, long pants, sweatshirts, jackets); how many wear glasses; how many are with children, and so on.

You can add another dimension to the game by guessing beforehand which will be the most prevalent color hat, mode of dress, etc. Or, based on the calculations, try to predict the look of the next people to join the line.

So, are you really just another face in the line, or does your family represent a new line of trendsetters?

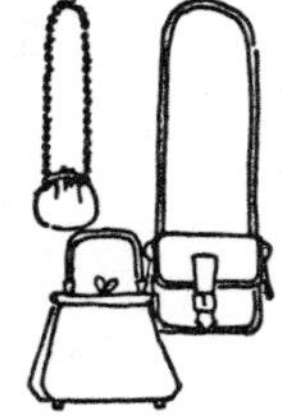

Observe the World

Mountain Climbing

It's said that climbing Mount Everest or the Matterhorn is one of the most daring feats that a mountaineer can undertake. The next time you and your kids are waiting, go on a climbing expedition of your own—using your imagination.

Anytime, Anyplace

Pick a tall building and imagine you're going to scale its heights. If you're inside, pretend that you're very tiny and you have to scale the lamp, or table, or chair.

Before you start climbing, figure out what kind of tools you'll need to make the climb. You will need some rope, backpacks for supplies, a harness for safety, and maybe some special tools like grappling hooks and rubber-soled shoes.

Then, as you climb, figure out how your expedition team will conquer each obstacle. What if you come to a huge window? Did you remember to bring suction cups? You can even get comical with your supplies: bang on the window until the building custodian brings you a toilet plunger, then tie the plunger to your leg and use it to traverse the glass.

By the time you get back to the ground, your wait will be over.

What an Imagination!

My Strangest Case

By Appointment

Here's a great way to pass some time in a waiting room—and, if it happens to be the waiting room of the doctor or dentist, defuse a little anxiety.

Take turns imagining that you're the doctor or dentist, and that you're relaying the strangest case of the day, like the person who swallowed a tuba and every time he exhaled he sounded like a foghorn. Perhaps as a dentist, you've seen a young fellow who brushed his teeth with white glue by mistake and couldn't open his mouth.

This activity works well in *any* waiting room situation. Perhaps you're waiting for an oil change or car repair; you and your child can take turns pretending you're the mechanic and describing oddities such as the person who locked an egg-salad sandwich in the glove compartment and lost the key.

You can also play this game by describing the problem and seeing if your child can guess what happened. You're bound to get some interesting answers. Perhaps the person who swallowed the tuba got a new job with the Coast Guard!

Name Game

Waiting to be Served

When you have kids, most of the places you go to eat don't make you wait long. Just shout into the clown's mouth and stop at the window. If you set your gastronomic sights higher, hold on to the menus after placing your order. Those folded papers are a ready-made word game for your kids.

Each player in the game takes a turn with the menu. Starting with the appetizers, the player uses the first selection to make a new word. "Crab Cakes," for example, can be used to make the word "brake."

The next player uses the same selection as his or her starting word. Play continues around the table, until one person can't form an original word. That player gets one mark (you can keep score by handing out sugar packets), then selects the next item on the menu.

The game can continue until your meal is served. The player with the fewest packets wins—besides, they always say that less sugar is better!

Name That Job

Anytime, Anyplace

Little kids are always wondering what mom and dad do during the day when they go off to work. This game introduces your kids to the world of work—and makes the time fly faster than a shoemaker's hammer.

To get started, one player chooses a person he or she sees working around them. It might, for example, be police officer.

After the person has been selected, the chooser gives one clue as to his or her identity. Your child might say, for example, "I am sitting in my car at the corner."

The other players take turns trying to guess which person the chooser has selected. If they can't guess after one clue, the chooser can give another clue. The round ends when one of the players correctly identifies the selected person.

To increase the challenge, put a limit on the number of clues that can be provided. If the other players can't find the person before reaching the last of the clues, the chooser gets to select another.

Hey, it's all in a day's work.

Observe the World

Name the Buildings

What an Imagination!

Your child has probably heard of the Statue of Liberty and the White House. But has she or he ever heard of the "Sugar Cube Building" or the "Trunkless Tree House" or the "Wedding Cake Tower?"

Next time you're walking to an appointment, ask your child to carefully observe the buildings and houses you pass, and think of names that would be appropriate for them. The moniker can describe the place's size, function, or height—or it can be just plain zany. For example, your child might label the local fire station, "The Dalmation Palace," the candy store might be, "Sugar Haven," and the gas station might get the name, "All-Cars-Can-Eat Restaurant."

Your child can also create histories of the buildings and houses based on their new names. Isn't it amazing: the Sugar Cube Building was built by an architect with a monumental sweet tooth!

What an Imagination!

Neighborhood Awards

Walking There

How many examples of excellence (or silliness) can you and your child find in your community during your next walk? Here's how you can find out, and hold your own Neighborhood Awards event.

Take a close look at the things (houses, buildings, pets, flowers, trees, and so on) that you pass as you're walking to an appointment or event, or while you're doing an errand on foot. When you find something that's really outstanding, recognize it with a spontaneous award. Perhaps the next-door neighbor's dog can win the "Best Golden Retriever Who Lives on This Block" award, a tree might be the "Maple That Houses the Most Birds," and the grocery store might earn the title, "Biggest Variety of Fruit Juice on the Street."

You and your child can also award prizes to vehicles that pass by as you're walking. You might encounter "The Shiniest Bicycle on the Beat," "Truck with the Longest Ladder," "Car with the Musical Horn," and the like. So what would you call the trucks that sell ice cream and Popsicles? How about "Very Cool."

What an Imagination!

Night and Day

Anytime, Anyplace

The world is a different place at night. Help your children explore those differences in their minds' eyes with this observation activity.

To start, ask your kids to pick out and name three things you can find outside during the day. Then, when you say "night," they have to name three things you can find outside at night.

You can make this activity more challenging by restricting your children's observations to their immediate surroundings. For example, if you're waiting in a line in the shoe store, see if they can imagine what the store would look like at night. During the day, the front door is open for customers. At night, the door is shut and locked. During the day, customers walk up and down the aisles. At night, the cleaning crew walks up and down the aisles. And so on.

Who knows, after playing this game a few times, your kids may never be afraid of the dark again!

No Countries

Anytime, Anyplace

What if the whole world were one big nation, and individual countries no longer existed? Ask your kids how we would:

Govern all the people in the world. Would we have government by one big world tribunal, or would we have a host of smaller tribunals? How would we make sure that everyone had fair representation?

Speak. Would everybody speak the same language? How would we decide which language was the official worldwide tongue? Would people be allowed to speak whichever language they wanted to? How could we steer them toward the official language?

Get along. How could people who have different customs, foods, clothing, regions, and even holidays learn to live in the same country with one another? Would we find it easier or more difficult to get along with each other?

Once your kids have thought about what it might be like to live in a world without individual countries, pose this question: Would you like to live in a world composed of just one country?

No Peeking

Here's a doodling activity that you and your child can go into with your eyes closed—as long as you plan to have some belly laughs when you're through.

Anytime, Anyplace

Make sure each of you has a piece of drawing paper and a pencil. One person calls out an object that you see (a clock, car, building, person, and so on). The other then tries to draw the object while keeping his or her eyes closed. When the drawing is finished, both of you look at the picture, and chuckle at the results.

For extra fun, suggest that your child draw a geometric shape (eyes open). Then suggest that he or she turn the shape into an object—with his or her eyes closed. For example, your child might start off drawing a rectangle and wind up adding three circles in a column inside. What is it? A traffic light perhaps. Or perhaps it's a front view of an electronic instrument (just add numbers and pointers to the circles). With this game, the truth only lies in the eyes of the beholder!

104 Object of the Story

Anytime, Anyplace

A few minutes of waiting time can easily be transformed into spellbinding storytelling time, providing you have a great storyteller—such as your child—on hand.

Choose an object in the waiting area, something that you spy while looking out the window, or something that a person is holding, and have your child make up a story about it. Perhaps your child can make the object the main character, endow it with magical properties, or turn it into a machine. For example, a paper clip can become Captain Paper Clip (a clipper skipper), a Planetary Radio Antennae (for picking up broadcasts from distant planets), or a Dust Zapper (for flicking dust off just about anything). Then see if your child can spin a story and bring it to a conclusion.

To further challenge your child's storytelling skills, choose another object while your child is in mid-narration, and have him or her incorporate it into the story line. So what do you suppose Captain Paper Clip will do when the Anti-Gravity Doorknob beams aboard?

Off-the-Cuff

Anytime, Anyplace

It takes a good orator to make an excellent speech on an important topic. But it takes a great orator—like your child—to give an extemporaneous speech about practically anything!

When you have some extra time, and your child is in a talkative mood, point to any object. Then have your child make a speech about it. You might specify a time limit—say, three minutes—during which your speech maker can talk about the object's history, who invented it, what earlier versions looked like, how it was first used, how it's used today, how it might be improved or adapted in the future, and so on.

For a real challenge, point to an obscure object such as the eraser at the end of a pencil, the plastic ends on a shoelace, or the T-shaped piece of plastic that holds a tag on a new item of clothing. See whether your child can make a full-length speech on the subject. Perhaps he or she can even tell you what the tag-holder is really called!

Oh, the Times!

Anytime, Anyplace

Now is the best time of your child's life! And here's how he or she can prove that it's the best time, period.

Appoint your child "Ambassador to All Time Travelers," whose task it is to greet visitors from other eras and explain why the present is the best time ever. Perhaps the first official duty is meeting with a couple from the Stone Age. Your ambassador/child might point out that now we have some great things that people didn't have back then, such as stoves, supermarkets, central heating, bicycles, electric lights, and so on.

Your child can then greet visitors from the future and explain why our "now" is even better than theirs. They might have figured out a way to cram an entire dinner into a small pill. But they'll never know the great experience of a burger, fries, and shake. And maybe we haven't figured out how to travel to Mars yet. But we sure have some great science fiction stories based on our ideas about Martians!

Curtain Call

On the Other Hand . . .

Anytime, Anyplace

What if everyone in the world drew with the "wrong" hand (the opposite of the hand he or she wrote with)? We'd have some very funny drawings, that's for sure!

Draw a simple picture and ask your child to copy it on another piece of paper. The hitch, of course, is that your child has to make the copy using his or her non-dominant hand (ambidextrous kids might want to try the exercise with either hand, but with their eyes closed). To really challenge your child's "wrong-hand" dexterity, add more complicated shapes and patterns to the original drawing, and then see whether your child can copy them, too. Your child can then try the drawing again, but this time, with his or her dominant hand. Isn't it amazing what a difference a hand makes?

And speaking of a-mazing, why not draw a maze on a blank sheet of paper? Using his or her non-dominant hand, your child then tries to draw a line through the maze without letting the pencil touch any of the walls. Now, give your child a hand for a great effort!

108 One-Inch Adventures

Anytime, Anyplace

What if your children were just one-inch tall? Ask how they would:

Navigate stairs. Perhaps your children would lower a string from a bannister and slide down it, or invent an elevator made from a paper cup and a string.

Eat. Since pots, pans, dishes, cups, and silverware would be too large, what would your kids eat and drink from instead? What foods would they eat, and what size would the portions be? Perhaps a single corn flake would constitute a whole meal!

Find clothing that fit. Since your kids' old clothes would be far too large, they would have to make a new wardrobe. What would they use for materials? Perhaps a cloth napkin would provide enough material to make a whole closetful of outfits.

Once your kids have thought about what life in miniature would be like, pose the following question: If it were possible to be an inch tall for a while, would you want to try it? Why or why not?

Opposites

Mirror, mirror on the wall, show me the opposite of everything you see. This abstract game takes you and your kids through a looking glass—you'll really need your thinking caps to play.

Anytime, Anyplace

Simply put, this is a grouping game, but it's challenging enough to keep older kids interested. Instead of separating objects you see into categories, as you would with younger children, the game here is to find objects that belong in two categories at the same time.

To get started, begin with a simple pair of categories—round and square. Then, look out the window or along the street. See that car? Round wheels, square windows. Or maybe you're inside—maybe waiting for the dentist. Look there—she has a round table covered with square magazines.

You can even turn this activity into a guessing game. Pick an object that you can see, one that accommodates two categories. That ice-cream truck parked at the side of the street—the motor is warm, but the treats inside are icy cold.

Spotting the little differences—that's the mark of a great observer.

Observe the World

Origins of Holidays

Anytime, Anyplace

Your child probably knows the origins of the major holidays. But what about some of the lesser-known ones?

Ask your child how Halloween, Groundhog Day, and Labor Day came about. When was the first Halloween? Whose idea was it? And how has it changed over the years? Try it with Mother's Day, Father's Day, or Flag Day—or any holiday or celebration that strikes your fancy.

You can also ask your children to invent holidays that they wish were on the calendar, such as Eat-a-Chocolate-Chip-Cookie-Day or Cloud Watching Day. How often would the holiday be celebrated? And what would the celebrations entail? Be sure to get information about the expected attire, the foods that would be eaten, and particular music that would be played or songs sung.

Hey, how about this one: Waiting Games Day—everyone spends fifteen minutes devising great things to do when you have to wait someplace. Be sure to take notes—you never know when you can put the ideas to good use!

Wise Kids

Origins of Things

Anytime, Anyplace

Stop! Look around you. . . . Do you know the origins of everything? Ask your child to tell you.

Look down at the ground. If you're outside, ask about concrete or asphalt. How is it made? Indoors, if you're on a wooden floor, see if your child can explain how do we go from tree trunks to floorboards. What about tile or linoleum? Carpeting?

What about building materials—steel, glass, limestone? Where do they come from, and how are they formed into the shapes we see? How about paint?

Then look at what people wear. Where does cotton or wool come from? How about the metals and stones in jewelry settings? Do they occur naturally? Do they "grow?" Do humans shape them?

Question everything, from the food you eat to the air you breathe. And don't forget to ask about the origins of time—that is, if you haven't gotten to where you're going already!

Out of this World

Anytime, Anyplace

What if it were possible to travel to other worlds in distant galaxies? Ask your kids how they would:

Decide which planets to visit. Would your kids stick close to home where the worlds were well-charted and found to be safe, or would they travel to the outer limits of the universe?

Choose where to live. If it were possible to live anywhere in the universe, how would your children choose which planet to make their primary residence? What would be the advantages and disadvantages of staying on earth?

Spend their vacations. Would your kids visit amusement parks, earthling relatives, and beaches when they had some time off from school, or would they explore the universe? What might other planets have to offer for vacationers that earth lacks?

Once your kids have thought about what it might be like to travel through the galaxy, pose this question: Would you want to visit other planets if you could?

Pace It Out

How big is the waiting room, restaurant lobby, or movie theater lobby? You'll find out (well, sort of) after your child does some custom measurements.

Anytime, Anyplace

First have your child pace out the room, or whatever you'd like measured. Then take a guess (unless you happen to have a ruler handy—the receptionist might) as to the length of each pace, in inches. See if your child can figure out the total number of inches. If he or she can divide by twelve, you'll know the answer in feet.

A younger kid will simply enjoy reporting that the room is thirty-five big steps long, or that a hallway is twenty-two giant steps. You can record the numbers on a notepad to make the entries "official."

Your younger child will also probably enjoy making a zany equivalency. For example, one big stride might be a dinostep, and a baby step might be a duck hop. So he or she might report that a room is ten dinosteps and one duck hop long.

Keep good notes—you might have some surprising news for the architect who designed the building!

Instant Game

Peaks of the World

Anytime, Anyplace

Why not give your children a pop quiz about the greatest mountains of the world? Here are some basic facts and figures you can use to test their knowledge.

What's the tallest mountain in the world? It's Mt. Everest, at 29,028 feet, located in the Himalayas, between Nepal and Tibet. Now, can your kids name the tallest mountains in other parts of the world, like:

Japan—Mt. Fuji, 12,389 feet
North America—Mt. McKinley, 20,320 feet (Alaska)
Europe—Mt. Blanc, 15,771 feet (France)
South America—Cerro Aconcagua, 23,034 feet (Andes, between Argentina and Chile)
Continental United States—Mt. Whitney, 14,491 feet (California)

For a twist, read the names of these mountains aloud, and see if your children can put them in size order and tell you where they are located.

For a bonus question, who were the first people to climb to the top of Mt. Everest? *Answer:* Edmund Hillary and Tenzing Norkay, in 1953.

Wise Kids

Pet Talk

Anytime, Anyplace

Whenever you see someone walking a pet, it's a good excuse for some fantasy play that will get some giggles out of your kids and make time pass faster than a cat running up a tree.

The trick here is for you and your child to get inside the pet's head. The game becomes an imaginary conversation as the dog (or ferret, cat, bear, bird, or whatever) goes loping down the street with its owner.

Dogs are especially fun because you can make up funny voices that fit the size and type of the dog. A "yip yip yipping" Chihuahua doesn't sound anything like a Great Dane.

So what does a dog say while walking down the street? Try commenting on the things the animal sees: "Oh, dee do dee do—look at that truck over there—wonder if it's a bone truck, sure could go for a bone right now. Had fun chasing that cat last night. Sure wish my human buddy would walk faster."

By the time you get home, your kids will be looking at their own pets in a whole new way!

Curtain Call

Pictures by Request

Anytime, Anyplace

Your child has probably created countless artistic masterpieces in his or her day. But has he or she ever created a picture to order, just for you? Here's how you might snag an original drawing, made by your child to your specifications. Perhaps you can even have it autographed!

Give your child paper and a pencil, and suggest that he or she draw an object (something you see while you're waiting, or perhaps something from your imagination). For instance, you might ask your child to draw a cow.

Then ask your child to incorporate additional features, one at a time. For example, you might say, "The cow has a bird on her tail." Then, once your child adds the bird, you say, "And the cow and the bird are both standing on a truck." After your child has drawn the truck you might continue, "And the truck is resting on a cloud," and so on.

You and your child will both undoubtedly be surprised at the results. Imagine drawing the first cloud-parked, truck-standing, cow-and-bird team!

Place That City

Do your kids know the cities of the world and the states or countries where they're located? Here's a starter list of cities and their locations—see how many your kids know, then add some of your own:

Anytime, Anyplace

Paris, France
Moscow, Russia
San Francisco, California
Tokyo, Japan
Shanghai, China
Taipei, Taiwan
Buenos Aires, Argentina
Juneau, Alaska
Peoria, Illinois
Detroit, Michigan
Los Angeles, California
Phoenix, Arizona
Santa Fe, New Mexico
Miami, Florida
San Juan, Puerto Rico
St. Louis, Missouri
Seattle, Washington
Chicago, Illinois
Philadelphia, Pennsylvania
Bombay, India
Copenhagen, Denmark
Berlin, Germany
Rome, Italy
Johannesburg, South Africa
Raleigh, North Carolina
Bogatá, Columbia
London, England
Lima, Peru
Toronto, Ontario, Canada

For a bonus: who can name the city where the president lives—and the state he hails from?

118 Places Unknown

Anytime, Anyplace

Just when you think the whole planet's been charted and explored from top to bottom, your child has discovered a previously unknown civilization at the farthest corner of the earth. And the best part is that you're the first reporter to interview your child and learn about his or her discovery!

Your child plays the part of the soon-to-be-famous explorer, while you get out the microphone (a rolled-up magazine or sheet of paper) and ask questions like: Where exactly is the new civilization? How did you happen to find it? What are the citizens like? How have they managed to remain cut off from the rest of civilization for so long? What language do the people speak? Did you have any trouble communicating with them? What foods do the people eat? How do they govern themselves? Do they have any machines that we haven't invented yet? Who are some of their more famous citizens? and so forth.

Then you can find out whether your child believes the civilization would benefit by joining the rest of the worldwide community.

Reporter-at-Large

Point Counterpoint (Little Kids)

It's no fun debating a child about when it's time to go to bed or what to eat. But debates about other topics can be a great way to pass the time. Try debating these topics with your younger child:

Anytime, Anyplace

1. What's the best ice-cream flavor?
2. Which is the best dinosaur?
3. What's the most unusual animal?
4. What is the best time of the day?
5. What is the best age to be?
6. What's the most fun thing for a kid to do?
7. What's the most fun thing for a grown-up to do?
8. Are baths important?
9. Are table manners important?
10. Is it better to be a big brother/sister or a little brother/sister?

Don't stop here, though—try this one: What's the most fun thing to do when you have to wait?

Wise Kids

Point Counterpoint (Older Kids)

Anytime, Anyplace

Your older child is probably great at defending his or her point of view when it comes to clothes, movies, and the like. See if he or she can apply some of that energy to topics such as:

1. Should we have zoos, or are zoos cruel to animals?
2. Should we spend money on exploring space when there are so many problems to be solved on earth?
3. Should we have more than one president of the United States?
4. Should kids be allowed to decide their own bed times?
5. Should kids be paid to do chores?
6. Would year-round school be better for kids?
7. Should kids be paid to get good grades?
8. Should kids be allowed to drive at whatever age they want?

There now, that should help you sharpen your debating skills, too!

Presidents Past and Present

121

Anytime, Anyplace

Your children can probably tell you the name of the current president of the United States. But how many of the other presidents can your kids name?

Using the list below, quiz your kids on U.S. presidents. You can simply see how many they can name, or try some more challenging questions like naming the first ten, the last ten, or, for real history buffs, all of them! You can also try questions like "who was president in 1864?"

1. George Washington 1789–97
2. John Adams 1797–1801
3. Thomas Jefferson 1801–09
4. James Madison 1809–17
5. James Monroe 1817–25
6. John Quincy Adams 1825–29
7. Andrew Jackson 1829–37
8. Martin Van Buren 1837–41
9. William Henry Harrison 1841
10 John Tyler 1841–1845
11. James Polk 1845–49
12. Zachary Taylor 1849–50
13. Millard Fillmore 1850–53
14. Franklin Pierce 1853–57
15. James Buchanan 1857–61
16. Abraham Lincoln 1861–65
17. Andrew Johnson 1865–69
18. Ulysses S. Grant 1869–77
19. Rutherford B. Hayes 1877–81
20. James A. Garfield 1881
21. Chester A. Arthur 1881–85
22. Grover Cleveland 1885–89
23. Benjamin Harrison 1889–93
24. Grover Cleveland 1893–97
25. William McKinley 1897–1901
26. Theodore Roosevelt 1901–09
27. William H. Taft 1909–13
28. Woodrow Wilson 1913–21
29. Warren G. Harding 1921–23
30. Calvin Coolidge 1923–29
31. Herbert Hoover 1929–33
32. Franklin D. Roosevelt 1933–45
33. Harry S. Truman 1945–53
34. Dwight D. Eisenhower 1953–61
35. John F. Kennedy 1961–63
36. Lyndon B. Johnson 1963–69
37. Richard M. Nixon 1969–74
38. Gerald R. Ford 1974–77
39. Jimmy Carter 1977–81
40. Ronald Reagan 1981–89
41. George Bush 1989–1993
42. Bill Clinton 1993–

And for a bonus: predict the next president of the U.S.A.!

Wise Kids

Prove It!

Anytime, Anyplace

What if you and your child were whisked back to an earlier time when many scientific principles hadn't been discovered yet? How could your kids convince their forbears of things that we know to be true today? Find out with this activity—and pass some waiting time.

Play the role of someone living five hundred years ago, then make a statement like, "The earth is flat, and if you go to the edge, you'll fall off." You might also proclaim, "The sky is a dome and the stars are light shining through little holes," or "Everyone knows that the sun revolves around the earth." How might your child prove such statements false?

Alternately, imagine that you're living two thousand years ago, and you believe that lightning and thunder are caused by angry gladiators in the sky. What does your child have to say about that?

Challenge your child's answers, but be open-minded—you might be surprised at what you learn!

Wise Kids

Quick Caricatures

What are your kids' impressions of how you look when you're waiting for something? Give them a pad of paper and a pencil, and find out!

Anytime, Anyplace

Decide which artist (your child, yourself, and others who are waiting with you) is going to sketch whom. Then agree on a time limit, such as five minutes, and see who can draw convincing caricatures. In addition to depicting the subjects' faces and bodies, caricatures might include "balloons" filled with words that the subjects are supposedly uttering or thinking.

As a variation, artists can draw their subjects without looking at them, then take turns revealing their masterpieces. They can also draw caricatures of their subjects as infants or young children, then see if others in the group can guess the subjects' identities.

Amazing—Dad even had glasses, wore ties, and told corny jokes when he was a toddler!

Quick Titles

Anytime, Anyplace

Perhaps Eugene O'Neill came up with the play title, *Long Day's Journey into Night* while he was waiting to take a trip (or a "journey"). In fact, your child can turn any waiting time into a new play or book title, and perhaps even come up with a plot.

In this activity, your child looks around, chooses something he or she sees (or is doing), and turns it into a title. A dog, or a picture of a dog, could turn into, "When Rover First Knew That the Aliens Had Finally Landed and Were *Not* Going Home."

See whether your child can develop his or her title into a plot. Perhaps he or she can incorporate other objects from your surroundings into the story. Friends and family who are waiting with you can be scripted into the plot, too.

Your child might instead want to offer you this challenge: he or she first tells you the story, and then you see whether or not you can suggest a great title. Sorry, *Long Day's Journey into Night* is already spoken for!

Rename the Eatery

Waiting to Be Served

What's in a restaurant's name? Just about everything you and your child need to know about the eating establishment—especially if *you* choose its name!

While you're waiting to be served, ask your child to suggest new names for the restaurant. The moniker can express your child's first impression of the restaurant (for example, "The Pizza Palace of Great Potential"). Or, if the restaurant is a tried-and-true family favorite, the name might be based on the types of foods that the restaurant offers ("The Something for Everyone Shop"), how often you eat there ("Once a Weekend Eatery"), the way you discovered it ("Grandma's Find of the Year"), what the furniture looks like ("Green Chair Cafe"), and so on.

Your child might also name the restaurant according to the "best" meal that's served there ("The Best House of Hamburgers"). If you have more than one young diner, make sure each child gets a chance to name the restaurant. Who knows—maybe the owners will take a hint from your family!

Repealing Newton's Law

Anytime, Anyplace

What if it were possible to make anti-gravity machines? Ask your kids how the machines would:

Change the world. Would it be necessary to have elevators or escalators? Or could people simply float up inside tubes to whatever floor they wanted to go and grab hold of "floor handles?" How about anti-gravity boots; perhaps runners could simply "anti-grav" hop over obstacles.

Lead to new forms of entertainment. Maybe we'd see the first "Anti-Grav Arena," where people bounced off foam ceilings, kind of like reverse bungee jumping. What other kids of games and thrills can your kids envision?

What If . . .

Avoid misuse of the devices. How could we prevent mishaps, such as people floating off into space, or anti-gravity machines accidentally turning on and disrupting a whole building or community?

Once your kids have thought about these issues, pose this question: Would you want an anti-gravity machine, if somebody offered to build one for you?

Report from Washington

Anytime, Anyplace

Imagine that you're a reporter and you're interviewing your child who's just finished meeting with the First Family of the United States!

Conduct the interview from "Washington, DC," which can be anyplace where you happen to be waiting with your child. Find out what his or her impression of the president was, what your child said to each member of the First Family, how the First Family was similar to and different from your family, what the White House looked like, and so on.

If your child met with the First Family to discuss specific issues, ask: What was the most pressing matter you discussed with First-Family members? Did you offer the First Family your opinions and suggestions? Was the First Family receptive to your ideas? and so on.

Also, remember to ask whether or not your child had the opportunity to meet the First Pet. So, is there anything especially presidential about the First Cat, or is a cat just a cat regardless of where he or she lives?

Reporter-at-Large

Restaurant Counts

Waiting to be Served

If your kids are peering around the restaurant waiting for the waitperson to take your order or bring your meal, then use this easy game to put their wandering eyes to good use!

The idea is for the players to predict such events as: how many people will walk in the door during the next two minutes; during the next four minutes, how many people will be seated; how many waiters or waitresses will emerge from the kitchen with food before the next person is seated? Whoever has the closest predictions gets to choose what will be counted during the next round.

Children take turns playing the role of the official tally keeper, jotting down the predictions and the actual outcomes on a paper place mat, napkin, or a notepad. They can also take turns being the official time keeper, calling out "start" and "stop" for the agreed-upon interval.

One thing you can count on—your kids will be too caught up in their predicting to notice that time is flying!

Restaurant Groups

Waiting to be Served

The dinner order is in. Now the long minutes of fidgeting begin. Before you resort to putting the sugar packets and condiments on the next table so your restless youngsters can't grab them, distract your kids with this quick "seek-and-find game."

Start the game by naming a category of objects, like shiny or round. Then, each person at the table must look around the restaurant and find something that fits into the category. If a player can't find a match, he or she sits out until the next round. The last player to be eliminated wins the round and gets to name the next category, or set a time limit and give each person a chance to be the category chooser.

This game works best if players stick to categories that are easily recognized, such as hot, cold, colors, food types, and clothing types.

Of course, some categories are dead giveaways. It never fails that when one of us says "slow," the first answer is "dinner!"

Rhyme Time

Anytime, Anyplace

Everybody is born a poet—and here's a way to show it.

You can play this game with one child or with a group of kids. To start, the first player announces a word. The next player has five seconds (you can allow more time) to say a word that rhymes with the original word. For example, if the first player says "car," the next player says something like "tar."

No repeats are allowed; each word has to be original. If you're playing with just one child, take turns thinking of words. If a group is playing, a player is eliminated if he or she can't think of a matching word. The last player left gets to pick the next word.

If you're playing with older kids, you can use words that are more difficult to find matches for: "boulder," "shoulder," and "older," for example. For very young children, stick with simple three- and four-letter words.

And when your kids stumble onto a word like "orange" or "purple," you'll just have to smile and make the best of it.

Roving Encyclopedia

Shopping and Erranding

So you're waiting for the elevator to arrive and it seems to be taking forever making its way down to the first floor—as elevators seem to do. What a perfect opportunity to get a lesson in "elevatorology" from your child.

Ask how an elevator works, and you'll likely get some surprising answers. But don't stop there. As you make your way toward your destination, ask your child to explain how all sorts of things work, from revolving doors and street sweepers to light bulbs and automatic teller machines (money actually does grow in machines, you see). Be sure to ask questions, too, as your expert gives out information.

Groups of kids can take turns giving explanations of things that you encounter, or, they can work together as a team to develop an explanation (silly or serious) that makes sense to them.

We're still a little uncertain how the giant boot and the boxing glove connect to the elevator buttons. But we're confident that we'll find out during an upcoming waiting game!

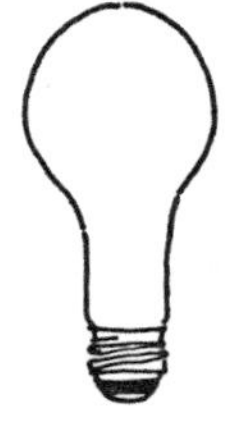

Wise Kids

132 Shoes Game

Waiting in Line

Everybody waiting in line generally has one thing in common. Well, two actually. Shoes! Your kids can have a great time passing the time cataloging all the different shoe types they see.

Start off by seeing how many different types of shoes your child can identify, such as high heels, sneakers, saddle shoes, loafers, sandals, boots, or whatever you're likely to see in your part of the country (make sure your kids stay within sight). Then ask for a count of each type and a determination of which is the most and least common.

To increase the challenge, have your shoe sleuths try to find shoe types of certain colors or locate laces or socks of certain colors or styles. You might for instance say, "Let's find a pair of brown sandals." "Who can spot a blue pair of running shoes and white socks?" or "The first person to locate the shoe gets to make the next 'find it' request."

For the supreme challenge, see if your kids can find the exact pairs of shoes they are wearing—complete with grass stains and chocolate ice-cream drips!

Observe the World

Shopping Cart Organizer

133

Shopping and Erranding

We all have to organize the foods in our grocery carts to some extent; otherwise, we're likely to end up with scrambled eggs on crushed loaves of bread. But did you know that shopping cart organizing can be a great way for your child to pass some time in the supermarket?

The simplest shopping cart organizer activity is to have your child arrange the goods so that similar items are grouped together. For example, you can challenge your child to place all the cans together, all the fruits in one corner, all the vegetables in another place, and so on.

In a more advanced version of the game, you specify a way of arranging the food that requires a bit more thought and creativity. You might suggest that your child organize the items according to color, texture, price, shape, and so on.

Now, then, how difficult would it be for your child to stack up everything that tastes sweet in one corner, and everything that tastes like broccoli in another?

134 Short to Tall

Anytime, Anyplace

Here's a quick way to put your observational powers to work—and watch the time fly!

To get the game going, start with the shortest object in your surroundings. It doesn't have to be small—something close to the ground will do. You can even start with the ground if you want, or with the sidewalk or street. The next player then picks an object that's a little taller. All of the players continue taking turns until one player can't find an object taller than the last one selected.

Think of it as that old game kids play with a baseball bat, putting one hand over the next until they reach the top of the handle. As you play, you may need to set up some rules; don't let kids jump from the street to the tallest skyscraper in a single turn.

If you're playing with your kids, and they manage to work all the way up to the tallest building downtown—well, you might have to keep a lookout for a helicopter or a plane flying by.

Sign Jumbles

Anytime, Anyplace

The word jumbles in the newspaper are one of our favorite ways to pass the time. But you don't need a newspaper to play word games—any sign will do.

To play, just turn your attention to the billboards, store displays, and traffic signs all around you. This is a great way to pass the time while waiting on a bus, or while stopped in traffic.

The object of the game is to see how many words can be made out of the letters on the sign. That stop sign on the corner, for example, contains the word *spot*. The marquee outside of the cafe holds the word *face*.

When you and your child play together, keep using the same sign until it stumps one of you. The last player to get a word from the sign is the winner.

If you're playing in the car, and you're stopped at a traffic light, keep going until the light turns green—but you'll have to think fast! Just how many words can you get out of that "Pedestrian Crossing" sign, anyway?

136

Sign Language

Anytime, Anyplace

In this storytelling activity, you don't even need to talk. All you need are nimble fingers—and some experience playing charades won't hurt.

To begin, you or your child thinks of a simple sentence to tell the other—without speaking. Start off with something easy, such as: "I like to eat ice cream."

To help your "listener" understand your meaning, you'll have to create signs and gestures. Pointing to yourself, for example, can mean "me." As for ice cream, well, you're on your own there.

Even very young children can play this game if you stick to very simple constructions. You can even build in some surprises, with sentences like "Let's go to the movies tomorrow!"

Groups can also have fun with this activity. Select a storyteller, while the others try to guess the message. For older kids, the messages can be more complex, or can consist of several sentences. Who knows? Wait long enough, and your kids might be able to convey the entire Gettysburg Address!

Signs and Stories

Here's a great way to stretch the imagination and shrink the waiting time.

While in the doctor's or dentist's office, or while waiting for a haircut, pick up a magazine from one of the tables. Your best choice is a magazine suitable for kids, but any magazine will do.

By Appointment

The first player closes his or her eyes, opens the magazine, and puts a finger on the page. Then, after opening his or her eyes, the player must read the word under his or her finger and make up an opening sentence using that word. For example, if you point to the word *bank*, you could start a story with: "One morning, Marvin the Mongoose decided to pay a visit to the bank."

The next player does the same thing but his or her sentence must continue the story. See what kind of story unfolds—it might just be Pulitzer prize-winning stuff!

What an Imagination!

138 Sky Watchers

Anytime, Anyplace

While many of us wait, we tend to look around, in front of us, and even at the ground. This simple game for very young kids will lift your spirits—and lift your eyes to the sky.

To play, everyone looks straight ahead. Someone gives a signal, then everyone looks up and call out the objects he or she sees in the sky. Birds, clouds, airplanes, and helicopters—they all count.

During the next round, your kids again look up in the sky, only this time they name all the colors that they see there. Encourage them to look everywhere; the sky, clouds, even the person washing the windows at the top of a building might be wearing a colorful pair of coveralls.

As an alternative, name a color and see if your children can find an object in the sky that matches the color. Or pick a number between one and five and see if your child can find that many objects in the sky.

Be careful, though: don't play so long that you get a stiff neck!

Observe the World

Solar System Kids

Anytime, Anyplace

Do your children love astronomy? They probably know how many planets there are, and lots of kids know that Jupiter is the largest in our solar system. How about having them try to name *all* of the planets, starting with the one closest to the sun? After they've named the planets correctly, have your children list them in *size* order, starting with the smallest.

Answer: Here's a list of the planets in our solar system, starting closest to the sun. The number shown for each planet gives its relative size, starting with the smallest (Mercury).

A. Mercury (1)
B. Venus (4)
C. Earth (5)
D. Mars (3)
E. Jupiter (9)
F. Saturn (8)
G. Uranus (7)
H. Neptune (6)
I. Pluto (2)

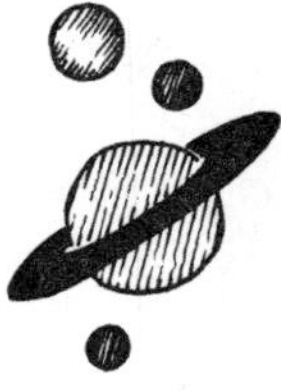

If your kids have gotten this far, they know a lot about the solar system, and they might be able to answer this bonus question: Between which two planets is the asteroid belt located? (answer: Mars & Jupiter)

Wise Kids

140 Songmaker

Anytime, Anyplace

Kids love to sing, but you don't need to carry around a songbook to keep them in tune. Some of the favorite songs in our family are the ones we made up ourselves.

Kids as young as five can help create songs if you borrow the tune from a song they already know. Once you have a tune, suggest a theme that your child is interested in.

A theme that works great for us is dinosaurs. We have songs about a stegosaurus sleeping in the bed, a duckbill hiding in the tree, even a tyrannosaurus who is growling in the yard. Whatever your kids are interested in, from trains to dolls, can be used to make the song.

Older kids will enjoy trying out different lyrics and rhymes to get the song just right. Take turns making up verses, and working with the other singers to build an entire song.

When you get home, you can write your songs down and illustrate them. If you have a tape player, record the finished songs—then you can play them in the car while traveling (and you won't forget the tune).

What an Imagination!

Soundalikes

Anytime, Anyplace

Are you and your child hearing double? It's likely that you will be once you've discovered these soundalike word games.

First you'll want to explain to your child that homonyms are two words that sound the same and are spelled the same, but mean two different things. Offer your child some examples of homonyms, such as the words *bat* (a flying rodent) and *bat* (as in baseball bat). Then ask your child to come up with other examples of homonyms.

Still waiting? Then tell your child that homophones are words that sound the same but are spelled differently. Provide some examples, such as *know* and *no*, and *whole* and *hole*, and see whether your child can offer some additional homophones.

Finally, if you have more time to pass, you can ask your child to invent some "sillophones." Sillophones are related to homophones, except that the second soundalike word doesn't exist until your child creates it. For example, "kid" and "cid" are sillophones; of course, a cid is an expert at inventing sillophones!

Sounds of Cities

Walking There

Every community has its own set of sounds. Next time you and your child are walking to an appointment or event, see how many sounds you can identify.

Listen quietly for a while, then ask your child to name some sounds and the soundmakers. For example, your child might hear engines humming in cars, wind rustling through trees, construction equipment working on building sites, and so on. Ask your child to describe each sound in detail, as well as its source.

As a variation, your child can describe a sound and challenge you to identify the object making it. How long will it take you to figure out that the "ocean's roar" is really the wind whistling through the leaves?

You and your child can also take turns imitating the sounds that you hear. Bet you didn't know that you had such a great bulldozer in you!

Space Odyssey

What if your children landed on a distant planet and didn't know the language or have the equipment to get back home? Ask how they would:

Anytime, Anyplace

Convince the aliens that earthlings are friendly. How would your kids describe what earthlings were like and how we feel, and convince the aliens that earthlings mean them no harm?

Find food and water. If they needed help getting something to eat and drink, how would your kids explain to the aliens what type of provisions they needed? If your kids had to buy food and water, what would they use for currency?

Find a way to get back home. What types of things might help your kids get back to earth? Where on the planet would your children look for those materials? How would they fashion the materials into a spacecraft?

Once your kids have thought about what it might be like to explore a distant planet, pose this question: If you could go, would you take the risk?

What If . . .

Space Voyage

Blast off to the planet of fun with this imaginative role-playing game that trades your car's earthbound wheels for fins and rocket engines.

Outer space is a fascinating subject for kids. By pretending that your car is a space vehicle, you give them a chance to talk about what they think space is like. They also get a chance to use the facts they have learned at school, such as what comets are made of, where asteroids belts are located, and the names of the planets.

As you move down the street, pretend you're moving farther into outer space. Other cars can be spaceships that you pass on the way to Pluto or beyond. Bicycles become comets, trucks turn into asteroids. Buildings turn into planets.

While you or whoever's driving acts as mission control, your kids play the role of astronauts. You can give them different tasks to perform, such as asking them to describe the comet you just passed or map a distant planet.

Just one thing—no space walks on this flight!

Speedy Word-Guessers

Waiting to Be Served

As this activity will show, if you have a pencil and a paper napkin or place mat (or a note pad), you're all set to pass some time until the waiter or waitress takes your order or brings your food to the table. (It's actually a take-off on the old "hangman" game, but in honor of the meal-time spirit, we've done away with the unpleasant metaphor).

Find a word on a menu, a sign on the wall, a decoration, advertising placard, and so on. Then draw enough blank lines for each letter. The players then take turns offering letters. Write down each correct letter in its proper place. For each incorrect guess, you write down a letter, in sequence, of the restaurant's name.

The object is for your kids to figure out the word before you spell out the entire name of the restaurant. (Note: if the name is exceptionally short or long, you might want to offer another name or word that you'll use to record incorrect guesses). The person who finishes the round gets to choose the next word, and the game continues—until the food arrives, at which point EVERYONE is a winner!

Sports Matching

Anytime, Anyplace

Sure your kids know that baseball requires bats, soccer requires shinguards, and you can't play basketball without a hoop on a backboard. But if you hand them a mallet and a wicket, do they know what the sport is? Test their sports knowledge with this quick quiz by reading items and terms from the list below and having your kids identify the sport. For a bonus, have them describe the object and how it's used, or define the term.

Try (rugby)
Goal kick (soccer)
Shortstop (baseball)
Pigskin (another name for a football)
Direct kick (soccer)
Love (tennis)
Wicket (cricket and croquet)
Face-off (ice and field hockey)
Baggataway (Original native American Indian name for lacrosse)
Scrum (rugby)
Deuce (tennis)
Letball (tennis)
Cager (basketball)
Century (cricket)
Hat trick (ice hockey and soccer)
Crosse (lacrosse)

Step-by-Step

We all know that every walk to an appointment or event begins with a single step. But did you know that the trick to playing a great walking game is to count how many steps you and your child actually take?

Pick a landmark that you'll pass—say, the fire hydrant or the stop sign a couple of blocks away. Then you and your child guess how many steps it will take you to reach that spot (each walker guesses the number of his or her own strides). See which of you comes closest to the number you guessed; the winner gets to choose the rules of the next game. Perhaps your new objective is to guess how many hops it will take to reach the oak tree, how many skips it will take to get to the bank, and so on.

As a variation, you and your child can pick a number of steps, and see whether you can reach a predetermined destination—say, a traffic light—in that number of strides. Okay, do you think that you and your child can take one hundred steps down a single block?

Subterraneans

Anytime, Anyplace

What if everything you see above the ground took place beneath the surface? What would it be like? Ask your kids how the subterranean folks would:

Build houses. Perhaps houses would hang from cave ceilings like giant stalactites. Would the cave houses be as comfortable as above-ground dwellings?

Grow and harvest food. Maybe farmers would toil in great underground fields, growing oversized mushrooms, while other vegetables would grow in huge lighted fields. What else can your child think of?

Travel about. People would also need some interesting gear to keep from bumping into walls. What would your kids suggest—perhaps flashlight shoes or beacon hats?

After your kids describe the subterranean world, pose this question: If you could live in an underground world, would you want to?

Sugar Packet Fun

What . . . no paper or crayons? Try these quick and easy games to keep your kids occupied until you're served.

Waiting to Be Served

Tic-Tac-Toe. Arrange the silverware in a tic-tac-toe grid, crossing two forks over two knives. Then use sugar or sweetener packets as the "X's" and "O's." If the table isn't stocked with two different types of packets, players can use one side of the packets to represent the "X's" and the other side for the "O's."

Edge Game. Two players on opposite sides of the table take turns tapping sugar packets across the table. The idea is to try to get your supply of packets as close to the edge as possible, without going over.

Sugar Pack Hockey. Players on opposite sides of the table each make a goal with silverware (an open "V" shape). Then they flick a sugar packet along the table top, trying to score a goal.

Sugar may not be great for our kids' teeth, but sugar packets are a great way to pass some meal time!

Instant Games

Sum It Up

Anytime, Anyplace

This quick math game requires a thinking cap, but not much else; play it whenever you have to wait.

To start, assign different values to items around you. If you're stuck in traffic, for example, you can say a car equals 1, a truck equals 2, and a building equals 3. Then, make up a simple math problem using those values, such as "Three trucks plus one car minus one building equals what?"

You can play inside, too, by assigning furniture and other objects different values. For older kids, make the problems more difficult by using subtraction or multiplication. If you set up ten separate values (0 through 9), kids can give their answers in code as well.

If your kids have a highly developed number sense, challenge them to devise their own numeral system, like the Roman numerals taught in school.

You can count on having fun with this game!

Super Math

Shopping and Erranding

Have you ever wondered what puts the "super" in the supermarket? Why, it's the fact that your child can become a super mathematician while you're getting your shopping done!

Let your young child practice math the easy way in the supermarket. You can have your child practice sums and differences by posing such problems as: what would happen if I have three apples in the bag, and I put four *more* apples in the bag? Or: what if I have seven cucumbers in the bag, but I put two of them back on the shelf?

Older children can keep a running total (based on rounded-off dollars and cents) of how much money your purchases cost. They might also keep track of how much it would cost to buy one of each type of food in an aisle, or even the whole supermarket. Now *that* will give your child practice in dealing with some astronomical numbers!

Surprise Drawings

Anytime, Anyplace

What can you and your child do together that you can't do on your own? If you have a notepad and pen and some time to fill, create a drawing of a "gorrizebra," of course!

First suggest a category (animals, vegetables, fruits, and so on). Then tear out two pages from your notebook, one for you and one for your child. Each of you draws half of a picture that belongs in the category on the top half of your piece of paper. Fold the paper to just cover what you've drawn, and have your child do the same with his or her's. Exchange drawings. Each of you then draws the bottom half of a picture (either the rest of the picture you started earlier or an entirely different drawing). Fold the papers again so that neither of you can see what's drawn on them. Once again exchange papers and unfold and name the drawings.

A half-gorilla, half-zebra drawing might be entitled, "Great Gorrizebra." A part lettuce, part onion might be a "Little Lettion." And a picture of half a banana combined with half an apple? How about, "a tasty fruit!"

Doodles to Go

Surviving the Stone Age

What if your children suddenly found themselves transported back in time to, say, prehistoric times? Ask how they would:

Anytime, Anyplace

Find and prepare food. What would your children eat (remind your kids that there were no fast-food restaurants in the Stone Age!)? How would they prepare and eat the food if they didn't have ovens, pots and pans, or dishes?

Make shelter. Where would your kids live? If your children couldn't find a ready-made dwelling, what building materials and tools would they use to build their own?

Communicate with fellow humans. How would your kids convince the locals that they weren't some weird kind of animal, and most importantly, that they were friendly?

Once your kids have thought about what it might be like to live in prehistoric times, pose this question: If you could go back in history and see what life was like thousands of years ago, would you?

Sweet Magic

Waiting to Be Served

This simple game delights the youngest children and makes slightly older kids feel proud that they can play. And it can outlast even the slowest kitchen!

Place several sugar or sweetener packets on the table. Then place a coin underneath one packet. Move the packets around, and see if your child can figure out where the coin is. Or have your child close his or her eyes while you hide the coin. How many guesses will it take to find it?

For added fun, you can maneuver the packets near the edge of the table and drop the coin into your lap. Play up the fact that the coin has apparently vanished—your kids will thrill to be in the presence of a great magician!

After playing this game for the twenty-eighth time, your kids may still be going strong. But *your* eyes may be the ones glued to the kitchen door!

Take a Trip

Anytime, Anyplace

If you and your child have a few minutes to spare, why not pack a bag for a trip to the North Pole, a faraway island, an imaginary planet, or anyplace else in the world?

To begin, choose either a destination that's familiar to your child (Grandma's house, a city you recently visited, a campsite, and so on) or one that's exotic (another country, a mystery island, even another time period or planet). Explain how long the two of you will be gone. Then have your child tell you which items he or she would pack for the trip and why. For example, your child might decide to take his or her warmest clothes and a camera to the North Pole. A weekend jaunt to a distant island, on the other hand, might require a bathing suit, T-shirts, shorts, and fishing gear.

You can up the challenge by telling your child that all items to be taken on the trip must fit into one paper shopping bag. That will certainly limit what you can take when you venture out of the solar system!

Tall Tales

Anytime, Anyplace

Remember those stories about Paul Bunyan and his blue ox named Babe? You and your kids can start your own folklore collection—and you don't even need a camp fire.

Say, for a minute, that you're waiting in line at the movie theater to buy tickets, and down the street, a big tractor trailer truck is unloading. That's all you need to start: "Did you ever hear about the truck that got stuck in the alley while making its deliveries?" you ask.

When your kids say "no," which of course they will, tell them how the truck was wedged between the buildings so tight that the dairy had to send over a dump truck full of butter. After covering the truck with the butter, a group of people was able to push it right out of the alley. But all the folks got so hungry pushing the truck that they covered it with maple syrup and ate it like a pancake.

Make your stories even more fun by putting yourself and your kids into the action. Wow! Who needs movies when you've got tales like these?

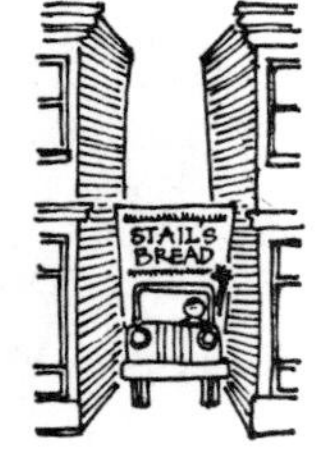

What an Imagination!

Team Efforts

So your child hasn't yet developed a taste for soccer? Well, then, why not have him or her get in on the ground floor of a brand new sport—one that he or she invents!

Anytime, Anyplace

Suggest to your child that he or she develop a never-before-played major league sport. Your junior sports inventor tells you whether the game is played by individuals or teams, how many teams play at once (who says it has to be two?), how many people play on each team, where the game is played (on ice, in a stadium, swimming pool, volcanic crater, and so on), how the game is divided (by innings, quarters, and so on), what the uniforms look like, what equipment is needed, and other important details.

Then your child can explain the rules of the game. For example, perhaps the object of "Snolleyball" is to hit a snowball across a volleyball net with tennis racquets, and the first player to squash the snowball has to make the next one.

Look out, Abner Doubleday! It looks as though baseball may soon be replaced by a brand new all-American pastime!

What an Imagination!

They Grow on Trees

Shopping and Erranding

There are so many fruits in the supermarket, you might think they grow on trees or something! But what types of trees do they grow on?

When you and your child are traversing the produce section in your local grocery store, take a moment to ask where the fruits come from. Your younger child probably has a sense that apples grow in orchards and that blueberries grow in bushes. If so, have him or her describe the trees and bushes (what they look like now and during various seasons), tell you which states they grow in, and so on.

Then see whether your child can tell you where some of the more exotic types of fruit, such as kiwis and mangos, originated (the former in New Zealand, the latter in India).

You might be surprised to learn that some fruits don't grow on trees at all—they grow in the ground like potatoes!

This Place in Time

What was it like to wait wherever you're waiting tens of thousands of years ago? And what will it be like the same amount of time in the future? Find out with this activity.

Anytime, Anyplace

Suggest a time period, past or future, then ask your chlid to tell you about the lay of the land (any new mountains, rivers, canyons, and so forth), the architecture (caves, tree houses, floating buildings), the people (what they're wearing, how their hair is styled, and so on), the sounds (are there wild animals or great interplanetary ship motors humming in the background?), the climate (whether it's hotter, colder, wetter, or dryer than in the present), and any strange sights, sounds, or sensations (erupting volcanos or "multimedia" sunsets that you can see, touch, hear, and smell), and other details that will give you a sense of your surroundings as they were or will be.

Wow, things were pretty wild back in the old days and sound pretty exotic in the future. But we like where we are right now!

What an Imagination!

Time Travelers

Anytime, Anyplace

What if it were possible to build a time machine and travel to the past or future? Ask your kids how they would:

Decide which times to visit.. Would it be more fun to visit the past or the future? What would they do once they got there?

Explain their presence. Would your kids let other people know that they were time travelers? What would the benefits and the dangers be of telling the truth?

Collect data. What kind of information could your kids gather about other times that would be useful to us now?

Change the past or the future. If your kids could travel through time, what would they change? What might the consequences of those changes be?

Once your kids have thought about what it might be like to travel through time, pose this question: Would you want to visit the past or the future, if it were possible?

Time Zones

161

What are people doing in various places of the world as you wait for whatever you're waiting for? That depends on where they're located, of course. See if your child can guess what time it is in the countries listed below, if it is 4:00 P.M. eastern standard time:

Anytime, Anyplace

Algiers, Algeria 9:00 P.M.
Amsterdam, Netherlands 9:00 P.M.
Bangkok, Thailand 3:00 A.M. (next day)
Cairo, Egypt 10:00 P.M.
Canton, China 4:00 A.M. (next day)
Copenhagen, Denmark 9:00 P.M.
Galapagos Islands 3:00 P.M.
Hong Kong 4:00 A.M. (next day)
Jakarta, Indonesia 3:00 A.M. (next day)
Khartoum, Sudan 10:00 P.M.
Melbourne, Australia 7:00 A.M. (next day)
Moscow, Russia 10:00 P.M.
Ottawa, Canada 3:00 P.M.
Reykjavík, Iceland 8:00 P.M.
Seoul, Korea 5:00 A.M. (next day)
Tegulcigalpa, Honduras 2:00 P.M.
Tokyo, Japan 5:00 A.M. (next day)
Vancouver, Canada, NOON
Zurich, Switzerland 9:00 P.M.

Wow, just think: if you were halfway around the world, all this waiting would be over and everybody would already be sound asleep!

Wise Kids

Touch of Gold

Anytime, Anyplace

What if your children had the Midas touch, and everything they touched turned to gold? Ask how they would:

Decide what they should and shouldn't touch. What things would your kids most enjoy turning into gold? What things are too important just the way they are to be turned into gold?

Spend their newfound wealth. What types of things would your children buy for themselves, for other family members, and for friends? Would your kids give any money away, and how would they decide which people or organizations should receive part of their wealth?

Feel about never being able to touch family members or pets. How would your children show people and pets affection if they couldn't hug or kiss them?

Once your kids have thought about what it might be like to have the Midas touch, pose this question: If you could have the power to turn everything you touched into gold, would you want it?

Tour Masters

Walking There

Maybe you've seen wherever you're going hundreds of times. But have you ever seen it through the eyes of your child? Ask your child to give you a tour while you're walking or driving along; you're sure to see things in a whole new way.

While you're walking, see how closely your child can look at the immediate environment and point out things that make the neighborhood or city unique. Encourage your child to look for the obvious, such as distinctive architecture or statues, as well as the more subtle. The door of the drug store, for example, might have interesting lettering or an unusual frame. Perhaps there's a flower box outside the drug store window filled with exceptionally brightly colored coleus or geraniums. Signs, notices on telephone poles, trees and shrubs, sidewalk benches, utility plate covers, and store names might all be gems waiting to be described.

With your child's keen eye and descriptive powers, your walk can become the adventure of a lifetime!

Observe the World

Traffic Cops

Gridlock Busters

Those eye-on-traffic reports you hear on the radio aren't much help when you're stuck in a rush-hour jam. But if you put your kid's eye on the traffic, you can make the wait an enjoyable experience.

Make traffic-watching into a game by asking your kids to name the different vehicles they see during a specified distance (for two blocks, for example, or from the store to home), or in a specified time period (before the next song on the radio ends).

As an alternative, you can name a specific kind of vehicle, such as an ambulance or police car, and ask your kids to see how many of them they can spot while you're waiting. If you don't have a large variety of vehicles to choose from, substitute colors instead, or make general categories like cars and trucks.

See if your kids can spot alternative modes of transportation, too, such as skateboards, bicycles, in-line skates, and mopeds.

Amazing how traffic is suddenly moving along!

Observe the World

Upside Down

Anytime, Anyplace

It's rumored (in our household, anyway), that when Leonardo da Vinci got stuck for artistic inspiration, he occasionally drew a picture upside down. In fact, that may just be why the *Mona Lisa*'s smile looks so weird—she was da Vinci's first attempt at upside-down drawing!

See whether your child can improve upon such primitive artistic efforts by using today's modern drawing tools (paper, pencil, and eraser). Give your child a subject (anything you can view while you're waiting), and see whether your child can draw it from the bottom up. For example, if your child is drawing a person, he or she starts with the model's shoes, moves up to the legs, then the arms, then the torso, then the neck, head, and hair. You might establish other tricky drawing rules, too: your child draws the right side of the subject and then the left side, or draws the details and then the outlines, and so on. You might be surprised at the results.

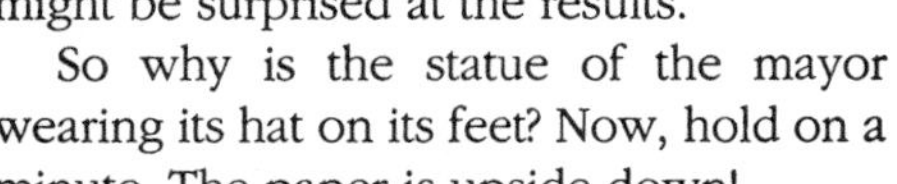

So why is the statue of the mayor wearing its hat on its feet? Now, hold on a minute. The paper is upside down!

Waiting Room Detectives

By Appointment

You might have visited whatever waiting room you're sitting in dozens of times. But without looking, do you know how many green square things are on the wall? Or what the smallest round thing on the ceiling is? You will after your kids engage in this waiting game activity!

Call out an attribute and a location, such as "square and floor," or "square and green and floor," then see how many objects your child or children can find that meet your criteria. If you have a group of kids, see if everyone comes up with the same number of things, or suggest that the whole troupe plays cooperatively, adding examples to a communal "pot."

You can extend the game by seeing how many instances of certain numbers or letters players can find, as well as how many examples they can find of things that move, things that require electricity, things that are made of wood, metal, and so forth.

The possibilities are limited only by your imaginations. Hopefully, though, by the time it's your appointment you'll just have scratched the surface!

Observe the World

Waiting Room Hot and Cold

By Appointment

There's nothing like a good game of hide-it to keep young kids from getting fidgety during a wait. And you can do it without causing a ruckus or turning the waiting room upside down.

Decide on something that is to be hidden, such as a scrap of paper, a particular magazine from the magazine rack, a brochure or pamphlet, and so on. Then have your child close his or her eyes while you place the mystery object out of sight, perhaps under the chair, under a stack of magazines, or inside a toy. As your child looks for the object, call out "hot" or "cold," as she gets closer to or farther from the hiding spot.

Once your child finds the object, reverse roles and have him or her hide the object from you, then call out "hot" or "cold" as you try to locate it.

Hey, look what you found—all those copies of *Green Eggs and Ham* behind the couch!

Observe the World

Waiting Room Scouts

By Appointment

There's probably a lot more going on in the waiting room than first meets the eye. Try this waiting game with your kids and see for yourself how the room is buzzing with activity!

Have your scouts keep track of the subtle activities in the room, in perhaps a five-minute period (you call out "start" and "stop"); how many people come into the room or leave the room, how many times people sit down and stand up, how many times the phone rings, how often someone coughs or sneezes, and so on.

You can add another dimension to the game by having your kids try to predict how many of the events they've been tracking will occur during another five-minute stretch. Whoever comes closest gets to be the time keeper for the next round.

We can't guess how many of your predictions will be right. But we can predict with certainty that time will fly as your kids watch the door, listen for the phone, and pay attention to life in the waiting room.

Observe the World

Waiting Room with a View

By Appointment

What would you see from the window of the waiting room if the building were suddenly transported to, say, the North Pole or a tropical rain forest? Find out with this activity, and pass some time while you're at it!

Start off by posing a location, say the jungle, the desert, or some other distinctive place. Then ask your children what kind of sights they'd likely see if they looked out the window. Ask about the kinds of animals that might saunter by, the kinds of plants that would likely be growing in the region, the terrain, what kind of weather they'd observe, and so on.

For older kids, you might suggest a city or country and focus on the people and culture. Ask about the clothing people wear, the foods they eat, and the language they speak.

And for a really fanciful view? The waiting room window can become the windshield of an interplanetary craft. What do your kids have to say about the inhabitants of Planet Doctuto? Hmm, they wear white coats and have stethoscopes around their necks . . . good thing they're friendly!

Observe the World

Waiting Words

Anytime, Anyplace

A picture might be worth a thousand words, but the place where you and your child are waiting is worth even more!

Choose a part of speech (noun or verb) and see how many words you and your child can come up with that are somehow associated with the place where you're waiting or the event you're anticipating. For example, if you're waiting for a train that will take you to Grandma's house, and the category is nouns, you and your child might compile a list like: Grandma, house, Cleveland, train, station, stop, seat, window, passenger, ticket, conductor, uniform, suitcase, wheels, tracks, scenery, and so on. A verb list might include: visit, travel, bring, ride, hold, sightsee, discover, listen, learn, eat, give, receive, and so on.

So how many words can you think of to describe how it feels to finally arrive? Excitement, happiness . . .

Waitperson of the Hour

Waiting to Be Served

And today's chef's surprise is the noodles with snake toes and broccoli wings, gently broiled at four thousand degrees for six days and served on a lush bed of tree bark!

If your kids are in a silly mood while you're waiting for a meal at a restaurant, let them take turns putting their energy to good use inventing and describing fantasy specials. To make it a team effort, each person adds an ingredient or cooking preparation.

Alternatively, your junior waitpeople can look at the actual menu and offer descriptions (real or imaginary) of each item—the ingredients, how the dish is prepared, its unique nutritional benefits, why it's the house special, and so on.

If you have a pad and pencil with you, the waitperson can also take down the orders, noting any special requests for food preparations or substitutions.

And speaking of substitutions, sorry, but there aren't any for the tree bark—that's what makes the dish so rich in Vitamin Z_{48}!

What an Imagination!

Water, Water Everywhere

Anytime, Anyplace

Any Huck Finn fan can tell you that Old Man River is the Mississippi. What do your children know about the other great rivers of the world? You can quiz your kids by asking them where these great rivers are and what ocean or sea they empty into. Then see if your kids can list them in size order (the lengths are listed for each one).

- Nile River (3470 miles) in North Africa and Egypt, runs into the Mediterranean Sea
- Mississippi River (2330 miles) in the central U.S., runs into the Gulf of Mexico
- Missouri River (2466 miles) in the central U.S., joins the Mississippi River
- Amazon River (3900 miles) in Peru and Brazil runs into the Atlantic Ocean
- Yangtze River (3400 miles) in China, runs into the East China Sea
- Colorado River (1450 miles) in southwestern U.S., runs into the Pacific Ocean

THE NILE

Wow—kinda makes you want to head for the drinking fountain.

Wise Kids

Weigh-In

How much does the average bunch of bananas weigh? According to a youngster we know, it weighs in at just under twenty pounds!

Shopping and Erranding

You can test your child's knowledge of fruit and vegetable weights (and imagination) during your next supermarket trip. Simply ask your child to guess how much three tomatoes, a pineapple, an eggplant, or another fruit or vegetable purchase might weigh. Then put the item or items you're planning to buy on the scale and see how close your child came.

Another way to play is to tell your child the total weight of a fruit or vegetable that you need, and see whether he or she can guess how many items it will take to make up that amount. For instance, you might say, "We need a pound of onions. How many onions do you think that will be?" When playing with older children, you can relate the questions to some simple math: "The onions cost a dollar for three pounds. How many onions will be a dollar's worth?" See how your kids' produce-shopping skills weigh in!

What a Character!

Anytime, Anyplace

There's nothing like meeting a famous storybook character to help pass the time while you're waiting. Have your child choose a favorite character from a book you've read together recently and improvise a scene.

Encourage your child to reveal even more about the character than the book does. For example, your child (in character) can tell you how he or she feels about other characters in the story, what life was like before the story started, what his or her plans for the future are, what people in the real world he or she would most like to meet and why, and so on.

You might select another character in the same book, and join your child in acting out a scene from the storybook. Or you might improvise a scene that wasn't in the book but should have been, like one in which the wolf tells Red Riding Hood how he's gotten separated from the pack, so Red Riding Hood goes to her grandmother's house to call the Wolf Rescue League!

What Am I?

Here's a game for creating an entire menagerie—with your hands and fingers.

Anytime, Anyplace

Each child and adult takes turns making animal shapes with his or her hands.

For example, hold your hand sideways, with your thumb pointing straight up. Presto—instant shark! By moving your pinky up and down, you open the shark's mouth.

A few simple changes turns your shark into an alligator. Curl your thumb so your hand is ready for saluting. Hold your hand out sideways. Now, when you separate your ring and middle finger, your alligator will open and close its mouth. Spiders are easy, too—just let your hands crawl across a table.

It's fun to combine your hands with your child's hands to make animals. Or make two animals that can converse with one another—a dog and a horse, for example.

Careful, though—you'll need a zookeeper if you keep this up!

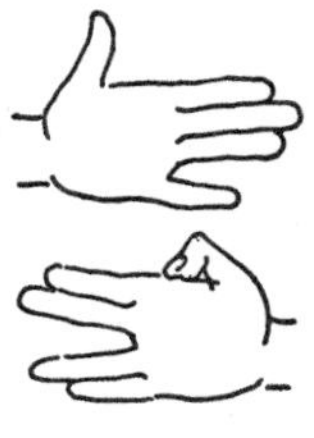

Curtain Call

176 What Am I Made Of?

Anytime, Anyplace

What goes into all those buildings, all that furniture, and all those cars and trucks you see all around you while you're waiting? Find out with this quick and easy activity.

The adult of the group starts the game off by naming a substance, such as "glass," "metal," or "wood." Then the kids in the group have to find and name an object that they can see from where they are that's made of the selected substance.

One of the best things about this game is that it can be played inside or outside, whether you're standing in a line, sitting in chairs, or walking to an appointment.

For older kids, you can combine materials into your clues using words like "and," "or," and "not." For example, "metal and plastic but not wood," might refer to a chair or table. As kids search for the item that fits your criteria, they build logical thinking skills.

And you thought it was all fun and games!

Observe the World

What Doesn't Belong (Little Kids)

Anytime, Anyplace

Do your younger kids enjoy placing things in categories? If so, they'll like this quick quiz. Read each list to your children, and have them explain why one item doesn't belong.

List 1: tree, flower, rock, grass (The rock doesn't belong because it isn't a plant.)

List 2: fork, potato, ice cream, carrot (A fork is not something to eat, so it doesn't belong.)

List 3: car, bus, chair, bicycle (Everything on this list is a form of transportation except a chair—it just sits there!)

List 4: brother, teacher, sister, father (Teacher doesn't belong—a teacher isn't a family member.)

List 5: red, yellow, paint, blue (Paint may be colorful, but it isn't a color and doesn't belong on this list.)

List 6: table, chair, sofa, bench (Don't sit on the table—it doesn't belong on this list.)

List 7: kitten, bunny, dog, snail (Snails aren't furry!)

If your children find their own reasons to come up with a different answer for any of these lists, all the better!

178

What Doesn't Belong (Older Kids)

Anytime, Anyplace

Older kids will enjoy testing their understanding of categories and relationships with this quick quiz. To play, read each list to your child and have him or her identify the item that doesn't belong and explain why it doesn't.

List 1: yogurt, milk, peanut butter, ice cream, butter (Peanut butter is the only food listed that is not a dairy product, so it doesn't belong.)

List 2: house, train station, library, grocery store, school (House doesn't belong—it's the only building on the list that people live in.)

List 3: snake, turtle, frog, iguana, alligator (All of these animals are reptiles except the frog, which is an amphibian.)

List 4: bicycle, wagon, scooter, sled, roller skates (All of the toys in this list have wheels except for the sled—it doesn't belong.)

Your children may have their own creative answers for these questions—an independent seven-year-old tester decided that the frog was the odd item on list 3 because, obviously, frogs hop!

What Kind of Food

Anytime, Anyplace

If you and your kids take a few minutes to look around, you'll see plenty of different shapes in the world. Have you ever thought how many of them look like food?

A tree can look a lot like a stalk of broccoli. If the tree is particularly tall, with its branches near the top, it might resemble a huge stalk of celery.

Clouds are really great giant food substitutes. Most of the time they look like marshmallows. But they can also look like bananas, doughnuts, or anything else your child's imagination suggests.

You can even take this game a step further and think about the things a giant might eat if he or she comes to town. A billboard might make a pretty good cracker—but what do you use for peanut butter? How about that cement mixer over there? Just turn it over and spread it with a small building—just right for an 11 o'clock snack.

Play this game while waiting in traffic on the way to a restaurant—the kids will have big appetites when they finally get to the table!

Observe the World

What Would Happen if Everybody Did It?

Anytime, Anyplace

City streets are filled with people waiting, walking, talking—doing all kinds of things. But these aren't usually group activities. You and your kids can have a lot of fun imagining what it would be like if everyone did the same thing at once.

For example, if you see someone walking a dog, say: "There's a man (or woman) walking the dog. What would happen if everybody did it?"

The answers your kids come up with can be hilarious: "There's one dog, and about a thousand leashes, and everybody on the street is trailing after the dog, jumping over each other and dodging fire hydrants!"

Or your child's answer might be a description of a thousand dogs, all walking at the same time, with all of their owners trailing after them. What a mess that would make!

The key to having fun with this storytelling game is to find activities with consequences that kids find easy to understand. It's a lesson in cause and effect—with the effect being a straight hit to the funny bone!

What an Imagination!

What Would They Do?

By Appointment

We've all thought it: you're stuck in some kind of difficult situation and you wonder what your favorite person—a friend you admire, even a storybook hero—would do in similar circumstances. The same idea can turn any wait into a game. And when you play in the doctor's office, the game can give your child the encouragement he or she needs to get through an anxious situation.

Here's how to get started. Take quick stock of your surroundings. Are you waiting to see the dentist? Ask your child what he or she thinks his or her favorite storybook character might do if he or she were visiting the dentist. What kind of dentist would Goldilocks visit? And what would the dentist say to Goldilocks? "Somebody's been sitting in my chair and it fits just right!"

What about the doctor? What kind of doctor would Mrs. Sprat visit? What would be her problem? "I just can't seem to lose any weight." "Well," the doctor might say, "have you tried making your dish run away with a spoon?"

What an Imagination!

What's Around the Corner?

Gridlock Busters

Anticipation, as this waiting game shows, is the key to a great activity involving children. Kids just *have* to know how the story will turn out.

As you're driving (or walking), you and your child try to guess what you'll see around the next corner or over the next hill. Your guesses can be anything from a kind of building or a kind of car to a person or animal. It might even be an activity—like a baseball game or some kids playing Frisbee, or perhaps construction at a new building site.

A fun twist to give this game is for one player to name an object he or she thinks is around the next corner, while the next player says "yes" or "no," depending on whether he or she thinks the first player's guess is correct or not. Then the tension mounts as everyone waits to find out what happens. Perhaps you'll be able to say that you've *really* seen the future!

Observe the World

What's for Dinner?

What are your family members having for dinner? While you and your family look at your menus, your child can second-guess your orders.

Waiting to Be Served

Each family member picks an item from the menu. Then your child guesses which food or beverage each person has chosen. Players might select their favorite foods, in which case, your child's knowledge of family members' tastes will come in handy. Or they might try to trick your child by choosing (at least, for the duration of the game) their least-favorite foods.

To increase the challenge, family members can choose an entire meal—say, an appetizer, vegetable, entree, drink, and dessert—instead of an individual item. Your child then tries to guess all of each player's choices. You might assign points to each category, such as one point for guessing the correct appetizer, two points for the vegetable, and so on. Then see how many points your child can rack up for accuracy when players actually order. So who would have guessed that Dad would order the octopus and a side dish of broccoli!

What's Next?

Shopping and Erranding

Wouldn't it be fun to get your supermarket shopping done, and at the same time, see whether or not you and your child are in tune with each other (and with whoever decides where groceries should be placed in the store)?

See whether you and your child can guess which foods (or other items) you'll find in the next supermarket aisle you're due to traverse. You can adjust the level of difficulty according to your child's age (or familiarity with the store). When playing with younger children, you might peek at each aisle's sign for clues; older kids might take "cold" guesses.

You and your child can match wits to see whether you agree about which products will be in the next aisle. The goal might be to see how many items that you both agree will be in the next aisle actually *are* in the next aisle, and how many times one or the other of you is "right." Of course, give yourselves credit for figuring out that the ice cream is in the frozen foods section!

Where Do I Live?

Anytime, Anyplace

Have you got a budding animal expert in your car? This quick-action trivia game will help your kids hone their zoological skills, without ever having to travel to the Serengeti.

To play, just name an animal. Your kids must name the animal's habitat within five seconds. For example, if you say "shark," your child can answer "ocean," or "water." Depending on the age of your children and their knowledge of animals and their habitats, the answers can be very specific or more general.

For very young children, stick to farm animals or pets with which they are familiar. Good choices here include cow, horse, rooster, turtle, frog, and cat.

With older kids, you can use more sophisticated animals, such as yaks (mountains of Tibet) and ocelots (small cat of the South and Central American rain forests). Anyone know where the Cuscus (a small marsupial) lives? (*Answer*: forests of Australia and New Zealand)

Where Does It Come From?

Anytime, Anyplace

Where does milk come from? Sure, it comes from the supermarket, but here's an opportunity for you and your child to review where things come from *before* we find them on the grocery store's shelves.

While you're waiting, give your child a list of things, and ask him or her where each item comes from. Besides milk, your list can include chocolate (which comes from cacao beans), wool (which we get from sheep), eggs (which come from chickens), paper (which we get from trees), diamonds (from carbon), pancake syrup (from maple trees), and so on.

Once your child gets to be an expert on where things come from, see whether he or she can cite the states or countries where items originate.

Add your own objects to the list, and then see whether your child can challenge *your* knowledge of origins. So, where do you suppose clever kids come from?

Where's the State?

All right, your kids know that Idaho is a state, but do they know where it is? Test their geographic acumen and pass the time with this simple trivia game.

Anytime, Anyplace

To start, name an area of the country. Your child must then name a state in that area. Say "west," for example, and kids have to say "California" or "Texas." The game also works well with cities, especially capitols.

Try playing the game in reverse. Name a city and see if your kids can name its home state. Or, name a state and see if your kids can name the part of the country where it lies: West, South, North, East.

Older kids can play a more sophisticated version. Name a mountain, river, lake, famous landmark, and so on, then see if your child can tell you what state it's located in. You might be surprised at some of the hidden truths of geography!

Wise Kids

Which Event Came First?

Anytime, Anyplace

This quick quiz about important historical dates will keep your kids on their toes. Just read events from this list and see if your kids can tell you which came first.

- World World I—1914 to 1918
- Railroad across North America—1869
- Civil War—1861 to 1865
- Women's Right to Vote—1920
- First U.S. manned space flight—1961
- World War II—1939 to 1945
- Bill of Rights—1791
- Moon landing—1969
- United Nations Created—1945
- George Washington Presidency—1789 to 1797
- Vikings explore North America—1000

For a bonus, ask for any details to the events, like what the United Nations does and who was the first person to set foot on the moon (Neil Armstrong).

Which Thing Came First?

Anytime, Anyplace

Your children are surrounded by gadgets, widgets, and inventions that affect almost everything they do—some very new, and some surprisingly old. Do your kids know when ice cream and bicycles were invented? Test their historical knowledge with this quiz.

Read this list of items to your kids and have them tell you which came first—you can read two at a time, or more for older children. After your children put the list in order, see how close they can come to getting the actual year for each invention.

- modern bicycle—1880
- ice cream—2000 B.C.
- Model T Ford—1908
- camera—1885
- airplane—1903
- electronic computer—1946
- hot-air balloon—1783
- television—1939
- wheel—about 3000 B.C.
- coins—600 B.C.
- paper—105

Fascinating—nearly 4,000 years of asking "One or two scoops!"

Wise Kids

Who Did It?

Anytime,
Anyplace

How much do your kids know about famous people in history? Here's a list you can quiz them on.

- Inventor of the lightning conductor—Benjamin Franklin, 1755
- Inventor of the telescope—Galileo, 1609
- First African American to play in major league baseball—Jackie Robinson, 1947
- Inventor of the electric light bulb—Thomas Edison, 1879
- First American woman in space—Sally Ride, 1983
- Inventors of the airplane—Orville and Wilbur Wright, 1903
- Inventor of the telephone—Alexander Graham Bell, 1876
- First man on moon—Neil Armstrong, 1969
- Creator of the Emancipation Proclamation, which freed slaves—Abraham Lincoln, 1862
- First woman to fly solo across the Atlantic—Amelia Earhart, 1932
- First president of the United States—George Washington, 1789
- First woman reporter—Nellie Bly, 1880's

When your kids have done their best with this list of famous people, try some more current ones by having them name the current president, the current vice president, the governor of your state, and of course, their principal!

Wise Kids

Who Knows What Fun Lurks . . .

Walking There

The world of shadows is its own place, where familiar objects like people, houses, and cars take on strange shapes. You and your kids can make that world your own with this playful activity.

The easiest way to play is to have your kids look for shadows on the ground, then associate them with the objects that make the image. This game can get really interesting in the evening hours, when image become elongated because of the low angle of the sun.

Alternatively let kids make their own shadow theater on the sidewalk. Hands can become animals or machines. Kids can also line up behind one another and make a multi-armed shadow.

Try standing in different places so that the heads of your shadows touch. Move your arms and legs to make a human shadow kaleidoscope—a shadowscope?

You can play these games whenever you have a sunny day and a long walk. After all, you've got to make play while the sun shines!

Observe the World

192 Who's Next?

Pick a door—any door. Right outside your car window, you and your kids will find more doors than you'll ever need to play this quick and easy time passer.

Each player—you and your child, or a group of kids—takes a turn guessing whether a man, woman, boy, or girl will be next to step out of the chosen door.

A variation of this game calls for each player to guess the color of an article of clothing that the next person through the door will wear.

Older kids can also keep score in another variation of this game by giving each color a different value, then taking turns looking at the door. Blue might be worth one point and red worth two, for example.

Finally, each player can guess what kind of clothes the next person out the door will be wearing. This can get pretty wild if someone guesses that "the next person will wear a pink dress," and then a man in a blue suit steps in!

Window Theater

Walking There

The curtain's going up on this fun activity that turns every walk into a Broadway premiere.

Store windows are filled with a cast of hundreds, players just waiting for some bright kids to give them something to say. Your kids take their cues from the clothes that the store mannequins are wearing. For example, if the clothes dummy is wearing a sports outfit, then it can be a famous athlete waiting for the big match, or granting interviews after winning the world championship.

This game can be even more fun if you spy a store display with more than one mannequin. Then your kids can make up stories as if the mannequins were characters in a play.

If your kids have trouble coming up with scenes for their silent cast, suggest favorite scenes from storybooks. Before you know it, the kids will be stealing the show. After all, they're no dummies!

What an Imagination!

Window Watchers

Anytime, Anyplace

If it's true that windows reflect the personality of a house, then there are plenty of buildings downtown with enough personality to stock a celebrity parade.

How much personality? To find out, count the windows. Pick a building—any building. Then, select a number of floors and ask your child to tell you how many windows are on those levels. For example, point to a building and ask: "How many windows are on the third, fourth, and fifth rows?"

Young kids will count the windows individually. But you can suggest shortcuts—if there are twelve windows on each floor, and there are three floors, then multiply twelve by three. If your kids don't have any trouble counting the panes, add to the challenge by linking math problems to the total count. For example, you might ask: "All of the windows on the fourth floor minus six is how many?"

Just don't make the math too complicated; otherwise your kids might say this activity is a real pane!

Observe the World

Windows on the World

If the waiting room has a window (you might ask the receptionist if a quick trip to a window in the hallway or stairway would be all right), you have everything you need to pass some quality waiting time.

By Appointment

Each person takes turns looking for a certain type of object on the street or sidewalk below, then sees if everyone else can find it. For younger kids, make sure that the chooser gives easy clues, like "I see something red with wheels on it." For an older child, you can be more subtle. If the same car has round lights and a rounded hood, the chooser might say, "I see something shaped like a frog. Its body is the same color as one of the stripes of the American flag, and its feet are made from a substance that grows inside certain rain forest trees."

Make sure that everyone gets a chance to select an object. Before your kids know it, you'll be calling out, "I see somebody waving that it's our turn to go in!"

Observe the World

With Apologies to Mr. Webster's

Anytime, Anyplace

Festoon, flabbergast, floccinaucinihilipilification. Would your child recognize these as real words (the last one means to trivialize something)?

Offer your kids a list of words that sound as if they could be made up—like "onomatopoeia" or "cacophonous." Present an equal number that are actaully made up, but sound real, like "flontipulate" or "diathonkuling." See if your kids can spot the ringers from the bona fide dictionary entries. (You might want to browse through the dictionary before you leave, or keep a "weird but true" list of words handy for passing the time. Look for entries like "siderdromophobia," which, believe it or not, means a fear of train travel.) Or, you might want to use words from your profession.

As a variation, ask your kids to guess at what the words mean. You're bound to learn some amazing facts—like how "floccinaucinihilipilification" has to do with the process of helping hippos take care of their teeth!

Wonderful Words (Little Kids)

Chances are, your young children have their own creative ideas about what new words might mean. Have some fun with their creativity and vocabulary with this word game.

Anytime, Anyplace

Read a word from the list below and ask which of the two definitions is correct (or, if neither is "right," ask for the "real" meaning). For convenience, we've listed the right answer first—be sure to change the order around as you go.

aardvark—anteater-like animal; small pointy shovel
lever—a bar or stick used for lifting something; a wall to hold back water
spatula—a kitchen tool for lifting or mixing food; a brush for scrubbing spots or stains
fender—the part of a car covering the wheel; tall, wavy grass
fife—small flute; fluffy stuff used by mice to make nests
kelp—brown seaweed; combination belt and suspenders
kimono—traditional Japanese robe; large lizard
mime—act out without words; large yellow flower
pantry—room for storing food or dishes; a patch for your jeans
rigid—stiff; very cold
kayak—small canoe-like boat; a big animal that looks like a furry cow

Wonderful Words (Older Kids)

Anytime, Anyplace

Do your older children surprise you with new words in their vocabulary every time you turn around? Have some fun and teach them a few new words with this quick vocabulary quiz!

Simply read the two definitions given for each word below, and see if your kids can pick the correct one (for convenience, we've listed the right answer first—be sure to change the order around as you go).

fennec—small African fox; tangy-tasting spice
parasol—a small umbrella; amusement park ride
cornice—building part that sticks out at the top of a wall; gravelly snow on ski slopes
deltoid—large muscle in your shoulder; triangular shaped meteor
isometrics—type of exercise; a way to measure trees
lamprey—type of eel; the light from a street lamp
paradox—a contradictory statement; a place to park two boats
quark—a sub-atomic particle; a small bird in the woodpecker family
fulcrum—the support point for a lever; the low point on a trail between two mountains.
transistor—a small electronic component; a tourist visitor from another country
wok—a bowl-shaped cooking pot; a path made by animals returning to a watering hole
zarf—cup holder; the front end of a canoe

Work for Hire

Anytime, Anyplace

How would your child like the job of cloud designer? What about volcano plumber? Well, both are up for grabs, at least during your waiting time.

Ask your child for some ideas about the zaniest jobs he or she can imagine. For instance, how about Face Painter—his or her job is to decorate people's faces at the coffee shop each morning before they go to work. Then there's Back Scratcher—someone who's always there for others whenever a back itch arises. Perhaps something truly ethereal, like "rain maker," whose duties also include deciding what color the rain (or snow or sleet) will be.

For each "job," have your child suggest appropriate pay (not necessarily cash), the hours of work, the kind of training that would be required, the kind of uniform or gear that would be worn, the dangers, the most gratifying part, and so forth.

Applications are now being accepted for park and playground evaluator. Anyone interested?

What an Imagination!

World Traveler

Anytime, Anyplace

Imagine what it would be like to travel the whole world with nothing but a pair of in-line skates, to get you over the land and a rubber raft to take you through the waterways? Meet somebody who actually saw the globe that way—your child!

Your child role-plays an intrepid explorer who packed extraordinarily lightly in preparation for a worldwide trip, and you play the part of a reporter who interviews the returning traveler. Here are some questions you might want to ask your child: Why did you take so little with you on the trip? How did you eat while you were traveling? What was your most exciting by-land adventure? Who were some of the most interesting people you met? What were the most surprising things you encountered? What were the biggest challenges of traveling?

Now that your child has returned, find out what he or she plans to do next. Perhaps your child's goals are pretty simple—like getting to a laundromat or visiting "the golden arches!"

Reporter-at-Large

Worstest Thing Possible

By Appointment

If the clock hands seem to be weighted down with rocks, try this activity while you wait for your appointment. It's bound to make time speed along as your kids flex their imaginations.

Think of all the possible things that someone might come to the doctor for, then think of which animal would have the worst time of it. Take a runny nose, for instance. That would be *something* for an elephant! Which animal would be the worst off with a stiff neck? A giraffe certainly wouldn't have fun! Continue the game so that you cover as many animal types as you can think of. Dinosaurs count, too—a T-Rex certainly wouldn't appreciate it if he had a sore throat.

You might also imagine what sorts of human treatments would be applied to the animals. A jumbo box of tissues for the elephant with the cold, an extra-long heating pad for the stiff-necked giraffe, and a chair-sized throat lozenge for T-Rex.

So you've fallen and skinned your knees—thank goodness you're not a millipede!

What an Imagination!

Zany Television Time

Anytime, Anyplace

It's half-time in the televised First International Waiting Bowl! The cameras are all on your child, who's responsible for providing entertainment and keeping you, the viewer, from switching channels. Suggest the following acts:

Mimes. How about some mime cheers—two, four, six, eight, how long will we have to wait . . . NOT MUCH LONGER!

Commerical Breaks. If you're in the dentist's waiting room, how about launching a new toothpaste? Perhaps your child will play the President of the United States and show off her bright, clean teeth.

News Flashes. What would be so important that it could interrupt a telecast of a national sports event? How about an ostrich that's escaped from the zoo (see Activity 57)?

Curtain Call

PSA's. Offer public service messages to viewers, such as the importance of flossing, eating right, and doing creative activities instead of watching TV—now *that's* public service!

Share Your Favorite Waiting Game Activities With Us

If you have any special ways of turning waiting time into great adventure time, please drop us a line. If we use them in future editions of this book, we'll be sure to credit you by name. Thanks! Send your ideas to:

Steve and Ruth Bennett
P.O. Box 382903
Cambridge, MA 02238-2903

All entries become the sole property of Steve and Ruth Bennett.

Index

USAGE CATEGORIES

Anytime, Anyplace

By Appointment

Gridlock Busters

Shopping and Erranding

Waiting in Line

Waiting to Be Served

Walking There

ACTIVITY TYPES

Curtain Call

Doodles to Go

Instant Games

Observe the World

Reporter-at-Large

What an Imagination!

What If . . .

Wise Kids

Word Wizards